DISSENTER ON THE BENCH

DISSE ON THE

RUTH BADER GINSBURG'S

Life & Work

NTER BENCH

By Victoria Ortiz

CLARION BOOKS | HOUGHTON MIFFLIN HARCOURT | BOSTON NEW YORK

CLARION BOOKS

3 Park Avenue, New York, New York 10016

Clarion Books is an imprint of
Houghton Mifflin Harcourt Publishing Company.

HMHBOOKS.COM

The text was set in Minion Pro.
Title lettering by Ellen Duda
Book design by Sharismar Rodriguez

Library of Congress Cataloging-in-Publication Data
Names: Ortiz, Victoria, 1942-, author.
Title: Dissenter on the bench : Ruth Bader Ginsburg's life and work / Victoria Ortiz.
Description: New York : Clarion Books, 2019.
Identifiers: LCCN 2018035167 | ISBN 9780544973640 (hardback)
Subjects: LCSH: Ginsburg, Ruth Bader | Judges—United States—Biography.
Women lawyers—United States—Biography. | Dissenting opinions—
United States. | United States. Supreme Court—Officials and employees.
Classification: LCC KF8745.G56 O78 2019 | DDC 347.73/2634—dc23
LC record available at https://lccn.loc.gov/2018035167

Manufactured in Malaysia
TWP 10 9 8 7 6 5 4 3 2 1
4500747414

To Jen,
whose endless supply of wisdom
and patience made this book possible

CONTENTS

ONE

A Teen Takes Her Case to the Supreme Court

SAVANA LEE REDDING was an honor-roll student at a middle school in Arizona. She was thirteen years old, a shy girl who liked nothing better than to work on her school projects, read books, and generally keep to herself. "Ever since I was little, I loved school," she remembered. "I never wanted to miss a day of it."

One October morning in 2003, the school's assistant principal pulled Savana out of her eighth-grade math class. He took her to his office and questioned her about items the school authorities had discovered in the possession of Marissa Glines, a classmate of Savana's, items that students were not allowed to have: prescription pills and an unidentified over-the-counter pill. Marissa Glines claimed that Savana had given her the forbidden pills. And another student reported to the assistant principal that Savana was planning to distribute pills to her fellow students at lunchtime that day.

Savana denied ever having such pills, denied ever giving pills to Marissa, and denied ever making plans to distribute pills to other students. Confident because she was telling the truth, Savana agreed to let the assistant principal and an administrative assistant search her backpack.

Savana Redding, 2003.

She knew they wouldn't find any pills. And indeed, they found no forbidden items in her backpack.

This was not the end of the story, however. The school authorities had only the unsupported accusations of two fellow students against Savana, the honor-roll student who had no disciplinary marks on her record. Even so, the assistant principal told the administrative assistant to take Savana to the nurse's office. He instructed the two women, the assistant and the nurse, to search Savana's clothing for the contraband pills. Now Savana was getting nervous, even though she had no pills on her. She was feeling pressured and helpless. In her words, "I didn't have an option. I was a little kid. I didn't have any idea how it would be handled."

Savana felt increasingly uncomfortable. The two school employees had her take off her jacket, socks, and shoes and found nothing incriminating. Then they ordered her to take off her black stretch pants with butterfly patches and her pink T-shirt. She complied reluctantly, and they found no pills in the seams of her garments. "Then they asked me to pull my bra out and to the side and shake it, exposing my breasts," she recalled. "Then they asked me to pull out my underwear and shake it. They also told me to pull the underwear out at the crotch and shake it, exposing my pelvic area. I was embarrassed and scared, but I felt I would be in more trouble if I did not do what they asked. I held my head down so that they could not see that I was about to cry."

Savana was told she could put her clothes back on, but she was not allowed to call her mother or return to her class. Instead, even after the assistant principal had been informed that no pills had been found, she was forced to sit outside his office for two and a half hours, in full view of any student or teacher who might pass by.

Savana couldn't tell her mother about what had happened until the end of the school day, when she went out to the car where her mother was waiting as she did every day to pick Savana up and take her home. Years later, Savana's mother, April Redding, wept at the memory of the helplessness she felt when she learned what had been done to her young daughter. "When Savana came out, she was very withdrawn. She came into the vehicle not wanting to look at me. Crying." The school authorities never explained their actions to Savana or her mother, and they never apologized for putting her through the traumatizing strip search of her clothing and body.

This experience was so devastating for Savana that she never returned to her school. She was heartbroken. "School had always been my safe place," she said later. "I loved school so much, and that's where I always felt the most loved by teachers and friends. I was always the really nice girl who was kind to everyone. I did all my assignments, made the Honor Roll and principal's Gold List every semester, and was well liked by the teachers."

Deeply angered by what had been done to her daughter, Savana's mother decided to fight against the intrusive school policy. First, Savana and her mom had to get legal help. They found it with the local Arizona chapter of the American Civil Liberties Union. The ACLU, as it is known, is a national organization that provides legal representation for people or groups whose constitutional rights and civil liberties have been threatened or violated by the government or some official agency. Savana and her mother began their lawsuit in federal district court. This is the trial-court level in the federal judiciary, which is the system that handles both criminal and civil cases under federal law.

In a federal *civil* case, an individual who believes she has been wronged because her constitutional rights have been violated can bring a lawsuit against a government official or an organization or a business entity. In a federal *criminal* case, a U.S. attorney, or federal prosecutor, files criminal charges against an individual or entity for allegedly violating a federal criminal statute, such as the one prohibiting counterfeiting. Federal civil cases involve matters governed by federal civil laws or the Constitution. Savana's case was a civil case against the school district that involved constitutional issues.

In the federal district court, Adam Wolf, Savana's attorney, argued that the school authorities had violated his young client's Fourth Amendment rights. This amendment of the U.S. Constitution guarantees the right to be free from unreasonable search and seizure by government agents, including public school employees. The attorney specifically argued that the unwarranted strip search of the thirteen-year-old honor student was unreasonable and illegal.

In preparing for this first stage of the legal process, Savana had to give an affidavit—a sworn statement—about the facts of the case. Throughout the months following the ordeal she had endured at her school, Savana had to repeat over and over again, in different settings and to different people—all of them strangers to her—the details of the ugly, humiliating strip-search incident. Even though this was very difficult for her and she would not be personally affected if she lost, Savana was determined to see her lawsuit through to the end. "It's more about other kids," she said. "I really don't want this to happen again. Ever."

Savana Redding, 2005.

Savana lost her case at the first level, the trial court, or district court. She appealed to a higher court, the Ninth Circuit Court of Appeals—the intermediate court, which is directly below the U.S. Supreme Court—for her circuit, or region. The federal courts are divided into twelve regional circuits, each representing a different geographical area of the nation. (There is also the Federal Circuit Court of Appeals, which can hear appeals from any part of the country. These cases involve international trade, patents and trademarks, and veterans' benefits, among others.) For example, the Ninth Circuit encompasses Alaska, Washington, Oregon, Idaho, Nevada, Arizona, Montana, and California. Each circuit contains a number of lower courts called district courts, where trials take place. Each circuit is headed up by a court of appeals, which is where losing parties may take their disappointment and appeal the district court's decision. If a case is lost at the circuit appeal level, the losing party can petition the

U.S. Supreme Court to hear a further appeal. Each year (called a term), that highest court in the land, the court of last resort, receives thousands of petitions for further appeal. However, the Supreme Court will take on fewer than one hundred cases per term.

In the Ninth Circuit Court of Appeals, Savana initially lost before a three-judge panel. Luckily, she got a second chance to appeal, this time to the appeals court sitting *en banc,* which meant her case would be heard by a larger group of judges, including the original three. Although they did not all agree, a majority of the judges who heard Savana's appeal thought her arguments were stronger than those of the school authorities. The court ruled that she had convincingly shown that the search of her clothes and body had violated her Fourth Amendment rights.

But the school authorities would not let it rest. They appealed this decision to the U.S. Supreme Court. The Supreme Court has the ultimate say on whether or not a person's rights have been violated, so this was the last possible place for Savana's lawyer to present his argument and hope for a final favorable decision. The lawyer would be assigned a date to deliver his best argument in support of Savana's claim that the school authorities had violated her constitutional rights.

On April 21, 2009, Savana and her mother sat in the courtroom of the U.S. Supreme Court in Washington, D.C. For Savana, the experience was, she recalled, "overwhelming." Because she was a party in the case, which was called *Safford Unified School District v. Redding,* she and her mom did not have to wait in line with the general public. This was a good thing, since hundreds of people were waiting for seats that day. Many were turned away after all the available seats were filled. But the Reddings were able to go right to the special seats reserved for the people directly involved in that morning's cases.

Facing Savana and her team as they sat waiting for oral arguments to begin was the impressive wooden bench—not really a bench, but rather a raised platform with a long, slightly curved mahogany desk behind which the nine Supreme Court justices would sit. These nine women and men are called *justices* to distinguish them from the judges in all the different types of local, state, and federal courts below them.

The raised bench, flanked by two American flags, was slightly higher than the public seating area and separated from it by a low wooden partition with a gate. Behind the justices' nine chairs were four white marble columns. The south and north walls were also marble, with sculpted friezes showing great historical lawgivers (Moses, Solomon, Confucius, Muhammad, Charlemagne, Napoleon, and John Marshall, among them) and allegorical figures such as Authority, Light of Wisdom, and Equity.

Savana's lawyer had described the setting and participants to her ahead of time. She knew that the person seated to the far right of the bench was the Supreme Court marshal, who was in charge of maintaining order and decorum in the courtroom. Almost on the dot of ten that morning, Savana watched as the marshal stood up and raised the gavel she held in her hand. Savana was expecting the very formal opening of the session as the nine justices, including Justice Ruth Bader Ginsburg, entered. Everyone stood when they heard the bang of the gavel, and the marshal said loudly:

> The Honorable, the Chief Justice and the Associate Justices of the Supreme Court of the United States. Oyez! Oyez! Oyez! All persons having business before the Honorable, the Supreme Court of the United States, are admonished to draw near and give their attention, for the Court is now sitting. God save the United States and this Honorable Court!

Supreme Court Justice Ruth Bader Ginsburg was born Joan Ruth Bader on March 15, 1933, a few days after Franklin Delano Roosevelt, known as FDR, was sworn in as the thirty-second president of the United States. This year was the worst of the Great Depression, a period when one in four Americans was unemployed. Across the Atlantic Ocean, shortly before Ruth was born, Adolf Hitler had been appointed the German chancellor of the Third Reich, ushering in the horrors of Nazism. A week after Joan Ruth's birth, the first concentration camp in Germany was established—Dachau. These camps, also known as extermination camps, were brutal, deadly places where the Nazis sent the men, women, and children whom they classified as enemies: Jews, Romani people (referred to as Gypsies), gays, and Jehovah's Witnesses, among others.

Joan Ruth Bader lived with her parents and older sister, Marilyn, in a modest apartment in Flatbush, a working-class neighborhood in Brooklyn, New York. Tragically, Marilyn died of meningitis when she was almost seven years old and Joan Ruth was not yet two. Essentially, Ruth grew up as an only child.

The two-family house the Bader family lived in was within walking distance of some of their closest relatives and of the public elementary and high schools Ruth would attend. When she started at Public School 238, which she attended from first grade through eighth grade, her parents learned that there were two other girls named Joan Ruth in her class and changed their daughter's name from Joan Ruth to Ruth Joan. The Baders' Flatbush neighborhood was lively, with Italian, Irish, and Jewish families living and working and playing side by side. Ruth's classmates and friends represented all three of these groups, making for a very rich social education for her and her peers.

Joan Ruth Bader, age two.

Until Ruth was four, her aunt, uncle, and little cousin Richard shared her family's apartment in a two-story gray building at 1584 East Ninth Street, a quiet street lined with trees. Richard was Ruth's "double cousin": his mother, Beatrice, and Ruth's mother, Celia, were sisters; his father, Benjamin, and Ruth's father, Nathan, were brothers. When Ruth and Richard were both babies, Ruth is said to have kicked Richard frequently, which led her older sister, Marilyn, to nickname her Kiki, pronounced "Kicky." The nickname stuck, and her closest friends and relatives called her by that affectionate name ever after.

The Baders' home.

Joan Ruth and Richard,
both age three.

Richard and Ruth were only three months apart in age and were very close. When his family moved out of the Baders' apartment, they went only a few blocks away, and the two friends continued to spend time together. In the streets of Brooklyn, they rode their bikes, played ball (sometimes tossing a tomato around instead of a ball) and hopscotch, and jumped rope. When they were a little older, Ruth and Richard taught each other to dance to the tunes they played on the Victrola, a record player, in the Baders' living room.

Celia was deeply committed to her daughter's education, both formal and informal. Together they attended young people's operas and classical music concerts and went to major museums and cultural centers in Brooklyn and Manhattan. Ruth's early experiences at the opera planted the seeds of a passion for that art form that would remain with her throughout her life.

Ruth and Richard, age ten or eleven.

Ruth was everything her mother wanted her to be. When, from time to time, her daughter did not perform as Celia thought she should, she let Ruth know. Ruth said later, "In the third grade I brought home a 'B' on my report card. She was horrified that I could be so lazy I couldn't even earn an 'A.'" In fact, the only truly bad grade Ruth ever received—a D—was for penmanship when she was just learning to write. She was left-handed, and her teacher had tried to force her to write with her right hand.

From the start, Ruth was a diligent, hard-working student. As early as elementary school, she developed the disciplined study habits that would lead to her great success there, in high school, and later in college. When she graduated from elementary school, she did so with a scholarship for outstanding achievement and service to the school. Ruth was also co-valedictorian at her elementary school graduation ceremony, on June 24, 1946. And she had the pleasure of playing the cello in the school orchestra on that memorable day. They performed "Land of Hope and Glory" and selections from Beethoven's Fifth Symphony.

Most important for Ruth's intellectual development was her introduction to the power of books. "One of my most pleasant memories," she would recall, "is of my mother reading to me." When Ruth was old enough to read on her own, she and her mother would go to the nearby public library. Ruth would sit and read while Celia went out to have her hair done. These weekly visits to the library soon turned Ruth into a prolific reader. Each week she signed out three, sometimes even five, books and happily devoured them at home. And since the library was in a building that also housed a Chinese restaurant, ever after her first visit there, Ruth associated the delicious aromas of Chinese cuisine with the deep pleasure she got from reading books.

Young Ruth Bader was always drawn to stories and books featuring strong female characters, like Jo March in *Little Women,* and even quirky ones like Mary Poppins. She was especially fond of the Nancy Drew books. Years later she would explain why she liked this girl character: "Nancy was a girl who did things. She was adventuresome, daring, and her boyfriend was a much more passive type than she was." Nancy Drew "was a girl . . . who could think for herself. The series made girls feel good, that they could be achievers and they didn't have to take a back seat or be wallflowers."

The goddess Athena was one of Ruth's favorites from the Greek legends. Not surprisingly, given the woman Ruth grew up to be, this inspiring deity symbolized wisdom and courage, strength and strategy, law and justice.

A real-life hero of Ruth's was Amelia Earhart, the first woman to fly solo from the United States to Europe. This pioneering aviator had disappeared over the Pacific Ocean in 1937, four years after Ruth was born. By the time Ruth was old enough to learn about Earhart, she was inspired by the aviator's example and admired her for breaking through gender barriers and advocating for women's equality.

Ruth didn't spend all her time buried in a book. In elementary school, she participated in the drama club, the school orchestra, and the eighth-grade devil-ball (a local version of dodgeball) tournament (her team won). When not at school, she hung out with a group of kids, including her cousin Richard, who remained a close friend through all their growing-up years. They did what kids in those days liked to do: play ball or jacks, ride their bikes, zip around on roller skates. Sometimes they would climb around the rooftops of the neighborhood houses, mischievously throwing gravel at unsuspecting passersby.

Ruth applied her strong academic skills to extracurricular activities that involved writing. She was the editor of P.S. 238's school newspaper, *Highway Herald,* and wrote articles for that paper. She wrote and published an editorial in the paper in June 1946, when she was about to graduate from eighth grade. Her essay focused on the importance of five historical documents: the Ten Commandments, the Magna Carta, the English Bill of Rights, the U.S. Constitution, and the Charter of the United Nations. Ruth ended her youthful editorial by calling on her classmates: "We children of public school age can do much to aid in the promotion of peace. We must try to train ourselves and those about us to live together with one another as good neighbors. It is the only way to secure the world against future wars and maintain an everlasting peace."

The lives of all Americans during the 1930s and 1940s were clouded by the Great Depression and then World War II. The war had officially started on September 1, 1939, when Ruth was six years old, and it officially ended during the spring and summer of 1945, when she was twelve. As a proud Jewish girl, raised in the traditions of her family's faith, Ruth was acutely aware of what was going on in Europe: the dark significance of Nazism, especially to Jews, and how the sufferings of the targeted victim groups were felt by all decent people. The atrocities being committed by the Nazis and their allies in Europe horrified her parents, teachers, and neighbors, who were appalled at the idea that such things might happen in the United States. They had heard stories of millions of people being rounded up by the Nazi authorities and sent to be murdered in concentration or extermination camps. By the end of the war, between 15 and 20 million people had died in the camps. Decades later Ruth would recall, "Nobody wanted to believe what was really happening."

This period saw the growth of overt anti-Semitism in the United States. Though the Brooklyn neighborhood where Ruth and her family lived had been a safe place, now some of the Baders' neighbors expressed hateful feelings toward them and other Jewish families. Some of the children with whom Ruth and her buddies played called their Jewish friends anti-Semitic names; some of the adults whispered ugly lies about Jews to neighborhood kids too naive to see through or challenge such fabrications. In Ruth Bader Ginsburg's words, "One could not help but be painfully aware of the antisemitism that existed in our world."

The families of both her parents had left Europe to escape the violence that was directed at Jews long before World War II erupted. Ruth was familiar with the stories of the organized massacres known as pogroms, in which bands of non-Jewish people in the Old World attacked and killed their Jewish neighbors. She also knew that there were fewer opportunities for Jews everywhere, even in the United States, because of anti-Semitism. She said later, "I have memories as a child, even before the war, of being in a car with my parents and passing a place in Pennsylvania, a resort with a sign out in front that read: 'No dogs or Jews allowed.'"

In 1946, when Ruth was thirteen years old and in eighth grade, she was on the editorial staff of the *Bulletin of the East Midwood Jewish Center,* the synagogue where she went on Sundays to learn more about the Jewish faith. At thirteen, she was confirmed there. If she had been a boy, she would have had a ceremonial coming-of-age celebration called a bar mitzvah, but only confirmation was available for girls. When she graduated from the Center, she wrote the lead article in the *Bulletin,* in which she decried the evils of the war in Europe, urging her readers "never to forget the horrors which our brethren were subjected to in Bergen-Belsen and other Nazi concentration camps." This short but profound piece was titled "One People" and put forth a principle that Ruth had learned in her studies of Judaism. This was the notion of *tikkun olam,* which in Hebrew means "the repairing of the world." According to this principle, it is each person's responsibility to repair those parts of society that are damaged by injustice or torn by inequality. Young Ruth wrote in 1946, "No one can feel free from danger and destruction until the many torn threads of civilization are bound together again."

Ruth's developing value system, which prized kindness, justice, and fairness for everyone, was honed and encouraged during the summers she spent at Camp Che-Na-Wah, a Jewish girls' camp in the Adirondack Mountains of New York. In the 1940s, it was not at all unusual for children, especially those living in urban areas, to be sent to day camps or sleep-away camps in rural surroundings. Many city parents felt that camp activities would prepare their children for civic and personal responsibilities in later life, as well as stimulate their imagination and help them to mature emotionally.

Camp Che-Na-Wah had been founded in 1923 by Ruth's uncle Sol "Chuck" Amster and her aunt Cornelia Schwartz Amster. Uncle Chuck was the brother of Ruth's mother, Celia. When Celia was fifteen and a recent high school graduate, she had helped financially to put Chuck through Cornell University. Aunt Cornelia had taken Ruth to concerts and other cultural events throughout her childhood. In their professional lives, Ruth's uncle and aunt were committed to providing the girls and young women who spent summer months at their camp with the freedom to "experience nature [and] group living and excel beyond their expectations."

Every summer from 1937, when she was four, until 1951, when she was eighteen and had completed her first year of college, Ruth Bader spent eight weeks at Camp Che-Na-Wah. Her experiences there were fundamental to the development of her character and leadership skills. She also undertook what would become a lifelong commitment to physical exercise and activity.

At Camp Che-Na-Wah, Ruth continued to develop in areas she already enjoyed and learned to excel in new ones. She took to the pursuits and routines of her days at camp with enthusiasm and a strong sense of belonging. The campers swam, canoed, rode horseback, participated in dramatics, and worked in arts and crafts. Many years later, when she was Justice Ginsburg and a grandmother, she visited the camp with her grandchildren and went out on the water with them, "while I can still paddle my own canoe," as she put it. She did remarkably well with the canoe, paddling quickly up and down.

Ruth was a leader at camp just as she always was at school. She functioned as the camp's unofficial "rabbi" and was charged with leading her fellow campers in thoughtful prayer at Saturday-morning services. As the "rabbi," she also gave her fellow campers presentations on important current events. Ruth began to develop her skills as a public speaker during those summers at camp. Her commitment to helping those less fortunate was strengthened and put into action during the organization and implementation of Camp Che-Na-Wah's annual charitable fundraiser.

By April 21, 2009, when the Supreme Court heard *Safford Unified School District v. Redding,* that once young, intense girl who had written about justice and fairness and cared deeply about freedom had become a black-robed jurist sitting very straight in her chair in the courtroom. Before Justice Ginsburg and her eight male colleagues ceremoniously entered and took their assigned seats, they had all spent time in their individual chambers—their private office suites—making their final preparations before entering the courtroom. For the last time, they looked over the notes each one of them had taken while reviewing the piles of paperwork that the lawyers for the two sides on the case had sent them. These included the briefs from each side—written, point-by-point arguments supporting the side represented and casting doubt on what the other side argued.

There were also exhibits, mainly documents such as copies of the

Ruth as "rabbi" at Camp Che-Na-Wah, addressing her fellow campers.

school's policies that were being challenged and of transcripts and decisions from the lower courts. There were also numerous documents called *amicus curiae* ("friend of the court") briefs. An *amicus curiae* brief is a written document that presents an argument for one side or the other in the hope that it will influence the court's decision. These had been sent to the justices by interested parties and organizations, offering either pro or con arguments related to the case at hand.

Justice Ginsburg, like her colleagues, was preparing herself to bring up areas of weakness she had found in the arguments of one side or the other, to ask for further clarification of parts of the case that were not clearly presented, and to challenge, if necessary, anything in the written arguments that she found particularly difficult to accept or to understand.

Before entering the courtroom to hear the day's oral arguments, the nine justices gathered in the robing room, where each of them had a locker. Special assistants were there to help them on with their traditional black robes. And then each justice shook the hand of every other justice before entering the courtroom.

On that April day, right in front of the bench, were the tables where Adam Wolf, Savana's lead attorney, and the attorney for the school district were sitting. The lectern in the center was where each of them would stand, facing the bench, to make their final oral argument to the court. The nine justices were seated according to seniority (the order in which they had been appointed to the court). Chief Justice John Roberts was in the center chair, the senior associate justice to his right, the second senior to his left. The remaining six justices were seated to his right or left, again according to seniority. Savana could see the tiny woman in the black robe with a fancy white collar sitting in the large chair second from the right up on the bench. Supreme Court Justice Ruth Bader Ginsburg, the only woman justice at the time, looked serious, almost majestic.

Savana's attorney had told her to expect an "active" or "hot" bench—in other words, many interruptions by the justices, who would ask questions of the attorneys and make comments that might reflect their own views on the case. Savana was anticipating that almost all the justices would interrupt the lawyers with lots of questions.

Even so, Savana didn't feel prepared for the experience that followed. She knew her own case inside out, of course, and she had very strong feelings about the injustice that had been committed against her. But she had not expected to hear lawyers and Supreme Court justices make jokes about serious matters that were central to her case. "My lawyers had advised me not to make any reactions to anything that was said," she remembered, "but it was really hard to do when I heard arguments from the other side that made it out to be no big deal or made me look like a delinquent. I sat like a stone and just listened and hoped the judges would see past that."

Savana was not the only person troubled by hearing the lawyers argue back and forth with the justices as if the case were a trivial matter not worth serious attention. Justice Ruth Bader Ginsburg, too, found it difficult to stomach the flippant manner in which her eight male colleagues and the male lawyers debated the details of the case.

After oral argument ended, when the justices discussed the case in conference behind closed doors, this jocular tone continued. As Justice Ginsburg later remembered it, "There were jokes about the boys in the locker room, and the boys unclothed in front of each other, and nobody thought anything of it. I said that thirteen is a vulnerable age for a girl, and a thirteen-year-old girl is not like a thirteen-year-old boy. This is overwhelming humiliation for her. There were no more jokes about boys in the locker room. I suppose my colleagues thought of their daughters, thought of their wives, and realized then that the point I was making was well-taken."

This time, Savana won her case. A little less than two months later, on June 25, 2009, the Supreme Court ruled that her rights under the Fourth Amendment had indeed been violated. She had been hoping that Justice Ginsburg "would talk some sense" to her colleagues, who, Savana felt, had "seemed to think being in your underwear was no big deal because they related it to the locker room." She had been expecting a closely divided vote of five in favor and four against, so when she learned that she had won by eight votes to one, she was overjoyed. She was particularly thrilled with Justice Ginsburg's additional concurring opinion and her powerful words confirming the majority's opinion; Justice Ginsburg declared that the

Savana Redding (right) with supporter Mary Beth Tinker at the time of the Supreme Court decision in her case, 2009.

assistant principal's treatment of young Savana was "abusive and it was not reasonable for him to believe that the law permitted it." Savana was jubilant: "She helped restore my faith in the justice system."

We can safely assume that when Justice Ruth Bader Ginsburg strongly urged her male colleagues to step out of their shoes and into Savana's, she tapped in to both her own experiences as a young girl and her long-held beliefs about justice and fairness. About her fellow justices, she said straightforwardly: "They have never been a thirteen-year-old girl. I don't think my colleagues, some of them, quite understand." Fortunately for Savana and for all schoolchildren from then on, Justice Ginsburg had persuaded all but one of the other justices to decide the case in Savana's favor.

TWO

STUDENTS HAVE RIGHTS TOO

S AVANA REDDING WAS not the first schoolgirl to have a traumatic encounter with school authorities. In 1999, about four years earlier, the sixteen-year-old high school junior Lindsay Earls had faced a very similar situation. In 1998, her Oklahoma high school had abruptly instituted a policy that required any student who wanted to be in band or chorus, or any other extracurricular group, to agree to undergo unannounced random drug testing.

Lindsay had never been involved in any drug activity, so she was not concerned about this drug-testing policy at first. She considered herself a "goody two-shoes" and was well known for her passion for many after-school activities. Lindsay realized that she—or any other student involved in extracurricular activities—might be subjected to random drug testing, and she felt strongly that the policy violated her right to privacy. But she wanted to continue in her choir, band choir, and academic team activities, so she reluctantly kept her objections to the random testing policy to herself.

Then, in Lindsay's junior year, she was randomly selected for the drug test. It was an experience she would never forget. One of the principal's assistants interrupted the class Lindsay was in and announced, in front of the other students and the teacher, that Lindsay had to go immediately to the school gym to be tested. The drug testing required Lindsay to go into the bathroom and urinate in a plastic vial while three of her teachers waited right outside the toilet stall. They were there to listen for "the normal sounds of urination." The teachers were supposed to examine and test the urine sample. So when Lindsay came out of the stall, she handed the vial to one of the teachers and was forced to watch as the teacher felt the vial "to ensure that it was the proper temperature" and held it up to the light "to inspect its color and clarity." She found it extremely embarrassing to be in such a personal situation with three teachers she saw in her classes every day.

After this humiliating experience, Lindsay and her family came to believe that the school's policy was in fact a serious violation of Lindsay's privacy rights. They found legal help at the Oklahoma chapter of the ACLU, the same national organization Savana would turn to a few years later. Through their attorney, Graham Boyd, the Earls family brought a lawsuit against the school district, challenging its hastily instituted random drug-testing policy. The suit charged the school authorities with violating Lindsay's and her fellow students' rights to freedom from unreasonable search and seizure under the Fourth Amendment to the Constitution, as Savana's would do four years later. Lindsay's attorney would argue that the drug testing at Lindsay's school was clearly an unreasonable search of her person and should be prohibited.

Lindsay believed her case was straightforward. As a high school junior and a member of the Cherokee Nation, Lindsay had always been active in her community and in her school's extracurricular activities, while maintaining a solid academic average. She was aware that in high school, being involved in activities outside the classroom was increasingly important. She wanted to apply to competitive colleges that required applicants to be well-rounded and involved in a variety of afterschool programs.

The lawsuit proceeded from the district court, where the trial was held first and where Lindsay lost, up to the next level, the U.S. Court of Appeals for the Tenth Circuit, which reversed the district court's decision, meaning Lindsay won at that level. The case then went to the U.S. Supreme Court, since the school district had not been happy with their loss in the court of appeals and had appealed that loss to the highest court.

Meanwhile, Lindsay had graduated from high school and had joined the freshman class at Dartmouth College in the fall of 2001. On March 19, 2002, during her college spring break, Lindsay was in Washington, D.C., in the courtroom of the U.S. Supreme Court, with her family. As Savana and her mother would do some years later, the Earls family was nervously waiting to witness the oral arguments in the case, *Board of Education of Independent School District No. 92 of Pottawatomie County v. Earls*. And they watched as the nine justices, at that time two of them women (Sandra Day O'Connor and Ruth Bader Ginsburg), walked solemnly into the courtroom and took their seats.

After all the waiting, the oral-argument part of her case was over in a flash, Lindsay remembered years later. "It was such an incredible day. When I think about it now, it almost feels like it was someone else's life!" She had been struck by the long line of people waiting to get into the courtroom. And at the end of the day, she was even more amazed by all the people waiting outside, especially so many young people, who wanted to shake her hand. "Afterwards, a group of kids came up and introduced themselves. They had driven up from their college in North Carolina and hadn't made it in time to get seats in the courtroom but stuck around to meet me. I was, and am still, so flattered. After all, I was just a regular kid who stood up for something I believed in."

Lindsay returned to Dartmouth College without knowing whether she had won or lost. Her case was now in nine pairs of hands, one pair of which belonged to the justice most likely to support Lindsay's position. Justice Ruth Bader Ginsburg was still the deep, critical thinker that she had been back in her growing-up days in Brooklyn. Like the young woman whose case she had just heard, Justice Ginsburg had valued both academics and afterschool activities in her high school years. Wouldn't she, too, have resented being subjected to a deeply embarrassing test for the privilege of playing in the orchestra or working on the school paper?

When Ruth Bader was a child, her parents taught her to love learning. Her mother had an inflexible approach to her schoolwork. "She made me toe the line. If I didn't have a perfect report card, she showed her disappointment." Pleasing her mother became especially important to Ruth when Celia was diagnosed with cervical cancer early in Ruth's first year of high school. Her mother's struggle with the disease shadowed Ruth's high school years, but this adversity made her all the more determined to achieve her goals. Many years later, Ruth would recall, "It was one of the most trying times in my life, but I knew my mother wanted me to study hard and get good grades and succeed in life, so that's what I did." Ruth knew that her mother liked to see her being a diligent and successful student. Celia increasingly had taken to her bed as her illness got worse, so Ruth did much of her high school homework sitting in her mother's room.

And succeed Ruth did. She was a highly accomplished student at Brooklyn's James Madison High School. A good friend of hers remembered, "[Ruth] was always prepared for class. She was often called on and

Ruth's mother, Celia Amster Bader.

participated. She always sat in the front, either because we were seated alphabetically, or perhaps because we were seated according to height!" (Throughout her education, Ruth was among the shortest in her class.) Another friend admired her humility: "She was very modest and didn't appear to be super self-confident. She never thought she did well on tests, but, of course, she always aced them."

Ruth's hard work and talents were recognized by her teachers, who encouraged her diligence and desire to learn. So highly regarded was she that Mr. Haas, the head of the school's English department, appointed her as his student aide. Only the top students in the school were chosen by teachers to be departmental aides. In this important advisory position, Justice Ginsburg would later explain, "I read books, and discussed them with him, to help him determine whether the books were suitable to include in the curriculum."

Ruth graduated from high school sixth out of a class of more than seven hundred students. She earned not only an Honorable Mention but also an English Scholarship Medal, the Parents' Association Award for Citizenship, and admission to the Round Table Forum of Honor. In addition, she was elected to Arista, a national honor society. She was ranked eighth among the twenty graduating seniors to receive New York State Scholarships to cover college tuition. But Ruth was unable to attend her own high school graduation. The night before that ceremony, on June 25, 1950, her mother, Celia Bader, died of cancer, days before her forty-eighth birthday. Ruth referred to her mother as "the bravest and strongest person I have known." Celia's strength and bravery were apparent in her attitude toward her devastating illness.

Celia Amster Bader was by all accounts an extremely talented woman. Had she lived in an era and an environment that permitted women to develop their potential to the fullest, she might have achieved professional status equal to her daughter's. She wanted her daughter to succeed, to be independent, but also to be a lady, which to her meant to hold fast to self-respect and exert self-control. "My mother influenced my life more than anyone else," recalled Ruth. "She was extremely intelligent, a prolific reader, caring and resourceful."

Her mother's influence, long illness, and early death inspired and strengthened in Ruth personality traits and ethical values such as persistence, stoicism, backbone, love of family, and commitment to doing good in the world. Ruth learned from her mother's experiences as well as her own about the ways in which some of the practices of Judaism held women back or set up unfair rules and expectations.

Ruth had been dismayed to learn as a child that she would not be eligible for a bar mitzvah when she turned thirteen because she was a girl. And when Celia died, leaving seventeen-year-old Ruth motherless, Ruth was angered because "the house was filled with women, but only men could participate in the *minyan*." Traditionally, when observant Jews gather for public worship, they may not begin the formal prayers unless ten men over the age of thirteen, known as a *minyan,* are present. Young Ruth thought it unfair that she and her female relatives and neighbors had to wait to say the prayers of mourning until there were enough men present for them to begin.

Judaism disappointed Ruth in other ways, too. She recalled conversations with her mother in which Celia described her own sense of betrayal by formal Judaism. "My mother had mixed memories of her Judaism because her father was ultra-Orthodox; she remembers [that] her eldest brother worked very hard to ride a bicycle and then his father caught him riding on the Sabbath and broke it to pieces."

This rigidity that allowed for the destruction of the bicycle seemed unpleasantly familiar to young Ruth when, while she was mourning her mother's death, she learned that the synagogue her family had been attending for years had now assigned them less prestigious seats for the High Holy Days. Why was this? Because her father was no longer able to contribute financially to the temple, since his business had suffered a serious decline after the death of his wife. Ruth understood: "I was seventeen when she died. My father fell apart. His business went to hell. It was the classic situation: she had been the strong woman behind the man."

Ruth's father, Nathan Bader, was a gentle and loving man. While his wife was strict with Ruth, he tended to spoil her. An immigrant from Russia, Nathan had very little formal education beyond the English classes he attended at night school when he was newly arrived. He worked hard all his life as a furrier, at times running his own small business, at other times working for someone else. He never made much money, but he managed to support his small family well enough so that Ruth never wanted for anything as she was growing up.

There is no doubt, though, that Ruth's lively intelligence was stimulated and cultivated from her earliest childhood primarily by her mother, whose own intellectual and academic talents when she was a girl had been thwarted by social and family traditions that discouraged girls from pursuing higher education. "My mother never had a chance in life," Ruth observed. "She was one of eight children. Although she had the best brain in the family and graduated from high school at fifteen, she had to work to put her big brother through college. When she married my father, she had to stop working or he would be thought of as less of a man."

Ruth's academic achievements were enhanced by her energetic and active participation in many activities outside the high school classroom, such as "playing [cello] in the school orchestra [and] going with my classmates to Ebbets Field on Dodgers Day to cheer for Jackie Robinson." Jackie Robinson was the first black player in major-league baseball.

Ruth also played the piano—she started taking lessons at the age of nine and continued them through high school and for a year when she was in college. She took up the cello so she could play in the school orchestra. Mr. Barnett, the orchestra director, gave her early lessons on a borrowed instrument. When she became adept, her family purchased a cello for her and also paid for private lessons. She always recalled with pleasure the experience of playing one instrument as part of a large group of musicians who, together, produced lovely music.

She was a member and treasurer of the Go-Getters, the high school pep squad that encouraged student attendance at school sporting events—she fondly remembered the black satin jacket with gold letters she and her fellow Go-Getters used to wear. She was a cheerleader and baton twirler of some competence, although she chipped one of her teeth with the baton; she helped put out the school yearbook; and she was the features editor of the school newspaper, the *Madison Highway*.

Ruth's classmates liked and admired her. In fact, she was a very popular girl, appreciated by her peers for her modesty and recognized for her high intelligence. Richard Salzman, a friend of hers who went on to become a judge on the District of Columbia Superior Court, remembered many years later that she was not at all "stuck up." Another friend described her as having "magnetism that drew people to her," while yet another identified a trait that was characteristic of the woman who later became a Supreme Court justice: "Ruth wouldn't speak unless she had something to say. She was always thinking. You might not even have realized she was listening until she'd say what was on her mind." In support of the high school's basketball team, the Mosketeers (named in honor of their coach, Jamie Moskowitz), former classmates recalled, "Ruth came to all the basketball games, sat right below (and behind) the basket with her friends, all of them laughing, having fun, and cheering on the ball players."

Testament to Ruth's popularity among her friends and to her modesty about her academic strength is the joking reference to her in the June 14, 1950, issue of the high school newspaper. By then Ruth had been admitted to prestigious Cornell University in Ithaca, New York. This was quite a feat for a young woman in those days, when almost all college students were men. The newspaper contained satirical verses about members of the graduating class; the entry for Ruth "predicted" that with a college degree she would be prepared to pluck chicken feathers in a poultry shop. It read:

So you're going to Cornell, Kiki, don't you snicker:
You may grow up to be a chicken flicker.

The powerful combination of strong academic achievement, well-rounded social and cultural engagement, and a commitment to thinking critically and doing the right thing made Ruth Bader someone to be reckoned with. She would not go along just to get along. When she felt someone had acted unfairly, she made a point of objecting to that behavior. When she questioned the fairness of someone's action, she probably disputed it in some way. Certainly, as her sense of values developed, she allowed herself to have thoughts and opinions that were at variance with what was considered the norm.

Ruth was not alone in embracing the right to disagree. All around her during the 1930s and 1940s, citizens were expressing their opinions about what was happening in the world, and doing so publicly, loudly, and emphatically.

As Ruth and her classmates approached their graduation day in 1950, public school teachers, including several at James Madison High School, were locked in a serious battle with the New York board of education. Because of a new law, called the Feinberg Law, all public school teachers were required to answer questions about their political beliefs, even though the U.S. Constitution protects people from having to defend against attacks on their opinions. The teachers were compelled to take a "loyalty oath" swearing their loyalty to the United States, even though this was a matter connected to a person's opinions and political beliefs. As a way of punishing those teachers who refused to take this "loyalty oath," the board of education refused to pay them for any work they did during afterschool activities. So the teachers stopped supervising extracurriculars, and the activities were then canceled for lack of supervision. The students were incensed. They blamed the board of education, not their beloved teachers.

Just two months before Ruth was to graduate in 1950, thousands of public school students in Brooklyn staged walkouts on several days, marching across the Manhattan Bridge to demonstrate in front of City Hall. These walkouts were the sensation of the city for the three or four days they lasted. Added to this, just as Ruth and her classmates were preparing to graduate and go on to college, eight public school teachers were suspended without pay by the board of education because they had refused to answer questions about their political beliefs and activities. They were ordered to leave their schools at the end of the same day on which they were informed of the suspensions.

A high school student climbed up to a window of James Madison High School seeking volunteers to join a walkout, April 1950.

These events helped open Ruth's eyes. Although she had no real power as a teenager to do anything about many of the injustices she saw around her, she could be angry and express disagreement. When she experienced the unfairness of the way women were viewed and treated in the context of her mother's death, she learned from it, and her resolve to object to such unfairness was strengthened. She moved away from many of the practices of Judaism because she would not accept the official views of women as being lesser than men.

Ruth Bader Ginsburg was always clear about the nature of her religious beliefs and her view of certain traditions. Although raised in a household where all the Jewish holidays and ceremonies were observed, she followed in her mother's footsteps, disappointed with the way girls and women were viewed and treated within Judaism. But Ruth was always fond of the Seders, or celebratory dinners, that her extended family hosted at Passover. During the Seder, the story was told of the heroic exodus, or flight, of the Jewish people from slavery in Egypt. Part of the ritual at the Seder was asking the Four Questions, which were traditionally intoned by the youngest child in attendance. Four times during the ceremonial meal, this child asks: "Why is tonight different from all other nights?" The answer each time explains the particular significance of the food eaten that evening and the way the family is gathered around the table, some sitting and some reclining—a posture implying freedom. "The best part of the Seder for me, the youngest child, was when I got to ask the questions," she recalled.

Ruth absorbed many of the teachings of Judaism that encouraged and celebrated a tradition of questioning, of challenging, and of disagreeing or dissenting. Learning about the history of the Jews, about their endless persecution across the world and the ways in which they persisted, resisted, and fought back, gave Ruth a solid foundation in dissent. She learned that justice and learning were central to being a strong human being, and that both these values were central to her Jewish heritage. Through her studies of Hebrew and of Jewish history, Ruth learned to value the lives of those who came before her, especially the Old Testament personage Deborah, not only as a woman, but as a general, a judge, and a prophet.

Once she became a judge and then a justice, Ruth Bader Ginsburg continued to revere Jewish history and teachings. She displayed on three walls of her Supreme Court chambers artistic renditions of the Hebrew command in Deuteronomy: *Tzedek, tzedek tirdof,* which means "Justice, justice shall you pursue."

And she understood clearly the deepest meaning of "to dissent," which means to dispute conventional or official opinions. Departing from a popularly held position was and is often frowned upon, even punished in certain settings. Certainly, when Ruth Bader Ginsburg was growing up, girls, young women, and even grown-up wives and mothers were generally instructed or pressured to agree with others at all costs. With the passage of time, Ruth Bader Ginsburg grew to value the Jewish tradition of dissent.

At the time of Lindsay Earls's case, Justice Ginsburg was one of two female justices on the Supreme Court. During the oral arguments in the case on March 19, 2002, Justice Ginsburg had already started to reveal her disagreement with much of what was being presented. The majority of the justices had seemed to indicate through their questions that they found the school's drug-testing policy acceptable and reasonable, and therefore constitutional. And by her questions, Justice Ginsburg had appeared to be taking the opposite position.

Once the oral-argument part of the process was over, the nine justices still had a lot of work to complete. On the Friday of each week when there were oral arguments, the nine justices gathered in the conference room with no one else present. At that time, each justice indicated how she or he planned to vote on each case. Then the most senior justice representing the majority position, that is, the one held by at least five of the nine justices, assigned the writing of that opinion to any one of the justices who agreed with it. Each justice assigned to write a majority opinion worked over the next several weeks on composing a draft. Then all the other justices had a chance to review it. At any point in the process, a justice could change position and join or leave the majority. Often, the justices in the minority would write one or more dissenting opinions explaining why they thought the majority opinion was wrong.

Three months after the Supreme Court argument, Lindsay and her family learned that they had lost their case, with five justices voting against them and four justices, including Ruth Bader Ginsburg, dissenting. It was devastating for the Earls family and their supporters, after all the energy so many people had put into preparing and arguing the case. The defeat was especially painful for Lindsay because her name was permanently attached to the case. In high school she had had a lot of problems with classmates who did not understand why she was rocking the boat by challenging the drug-testing policy. There had been meanness and ostracizing and name-calling, although her closest friends remained true.

Lindsay Earls with Justice Ginsburg in 2015, thirteen years after the Supreme Court heard her case.

Lindsay was particularly dismayed that Justice Clarence Thomas had written the majority opinion. Apart from her chagrin at the opinion itself, she had noticed that Justice Thomas looked as if he was asleep throughout the entire oral argument. In her words, "I thought he was just that bored by my case!"

But despite the disappointing news for Lindsay and her family, they knew that their lawyers' arguments had had an impact on four of the justices. These dissenters had stood up for the Earls family and all others like them. They had pointed to an injustice and had tried to put it right. Justice Ginsburg, in her dissent, characterized the school district's drug-testing policy as "not reasonable . . . capricious, even perverse." And, on a personal level, Lindsay observed, "Justice Ginsburg's dissent made me feel like I truly had a friend on the Supreme Court. There was SOMEONE who listened to my story and valued my experience, instead of brushing me off for being just a kid."

THREE

STANDING UP FOR FREE EXPRESSION

JOE FREDERICK HAD moved with his father from Seattle, Washington, to Juneau, Alaska, before the 2001–2002 school year. Like any high-schooler joining a class of students who had all grown up together, eighteen-year-old Joe felt a bit like a fish out of water as a senior at his new school. He missed his old friends and longed for his familiar hangouts. Joe had generally performed well in his classes at his Seattle high school. In fact, he was academically ready to be done with high school by the end of his junior year, having completed enough credits to graduate. In some ways he was immature for his age, and his father felt that a final year of high school before starting college would help him grow up and give him more of a focus on the future.

Rather than trying to fit in with the majority, Joe found it easier and more comfortable to become part of the "out crowd," known more for misbehavior than for academic prowess. But he was fascinated by constitutional law. In his junior year in Seattle, he had taken a class called American Justice and had relished delving further into subjects that had been introduced in earlier civics classes. He liked learning in greater depth about the civil rights all citizens enjoyed, as detailed in the first ten amendments to the U.S. Constitution. He was very serious about his commitment to these basic civil rights and fearless when it came to standing up for his rights and those of others.

Joe became quite well-known to the school administrators at his Juneau high school as a student who did not readily obey their orders. When the vice principal told him that he could not sit in the student commons area—even quietly reading a book—if no adults were present, Joe argued with him, insisting that he had a constitutional right to be there. The vice principal did not agree and called in the Juneau police, two of whom escorted Joe from the building.

On another occasion, Joe refused to stand for the Pledge of Allegiance at the start of the school day, turning his chair around so that his back was to the flag. The school authorities threatened him with a five-day suspension, even though, almost sixty years earlier, the Supreme Court had ruled that public schools may not force students to recite the Pledge of Allegiance. The Juneau school authorities ultimately changed their minds when Joe's father protested that the suspension would be a violation of Joe's constitutionally protected rights of free expression.

The relationship between Joe Frederick and the Juneau high school administrators was strained, to say the least. They found him a handful, with his in-your-face objections to what he saw as the school's infringement on his rights. Joe viewed the principal and her colleagues as oppressors when they sought to enforce school regulations in ways they believed to be evenhanded. Joe was also fast becoming known to teachers and administrators as an inveterate instigator and prankster who took great pleasure in provoking those around him. A classmate described him as "a kid who liked to push buttons."

It was in this context that Joe Frederick decided to come up with some action that, in his words, "would clearly be constitutionally protected speech and speech that would be funny and at the same time embarrass the high school administration." At first, Joe had no specific ideas about when he would take this action, where it would occur, or what it would involve.

Suddenly, the "when" presented itself almost ready-made. It was announced that on January 24, 2002, the Olympic torch relay, sponsored by the Coca-Cola Company, would go through Juneau—down its main street, where the high school was located. What a perfect occasion for his constitutionally protected gesture!

The "where" became obvious once the school authorities shared their plans. They would be letting students leave the school and stand on the other side of Glacier Avenue, directly in front of the high school building, to cheer on the passing Olympic torchbearer. Joe and his friends would be standing across the street from the school, off school property, where, they believed, they would be beyond the reach of the school's authority.

All that was left for Joe and friends to figure out was the "what." What was the most powerful statement they could make that would probably annoy the school but would be clearly protected by the free-speech clause in the First Amendment and would be funny at the same time? They wanted their gesture to be eye-catching as well. CNN's TV news cameras would be there covering the Olympic relay, so the students' action would likely be carried out "in front of the entire nation!"

The action itself was determined when Joe's girlfriend, Makana, noticed a sticker on a snowboard that read "Bong Hits for Jesus" and found it funny. When she showed Joe the sticker, he realized he had his protest statement right under his nose. "This was the protected speech and parody that was perfect for the planned free speech experiment," he recalled. "We would unfurl a banner on private property and across the street from the high school during the running of the Olympic Torch, which was being covered by CNN." As the Olympic relay passed along Glacier Avenue, Joe and thirteen of his friends unfurled the fourteen-foot paper banner on which they had written with duct tape the words "Bong Hits 4 Jesus."

Joe's "free speech experiment" met with varying reactions. The other students were not particularly impressed, if they even noticed. Since the students were not in school, many of them were engaged in snowball fights and other horseplay and not paying much attention to what was going on around them. Those students who did notice the banner, according to a classmate, "thought it was dumb."

The school administrators, on the other hand, reacted almost immediately. Accompanied by the assistant principal and a school custodian, high school principal Deborah Morse ran across the street and ripped the banner from the students' hands. Thirteen of them let go of the banner and stepped away from the confrontation. Joe remained, protesting vehemently: "What about my First Amendment rights of free speech?" According to Joe, the principal replied, "High school students do not have free speech."

Joe's classmates watched this exchange from the sidelines. They were not impressed by the school authorities. A student reported, "People were mostly amused by the way the administrators reacted, how they got on their walkie-talkies and called for backup."

Back in the principal's office, Joe continued to argue for his right to express himself freely, and Principal Morse continued to maintain that as a high school student, Joe had no constitutional rights. She was not exactly correct on this detail. In a landmark case forty years earlier involving junior and senior high school students who were expressing their opposition to the war in Vietnam by wearing black armbands, the Supreme

Court had stated clearly, "Students do not shed their constitutional rights to freedom of speech or expression at the schoolhouse gate."

But Principal Morse's office was not a courtroom, and in it, her rules were law. Joe Frederick's banner, which seemed to the principal to be sending a pro-drug message, and his insistence that his free-speech rights be respected, led Principal Morse to suspend him for ten days and to bar him completely from school property.

Joe Frederick immediately contacted the local ACLU lawyers and asked them to represent him in a lawsuit against Principal Deborah Morse and the school board. He was fortunate enough to be assisted in his suit by attorney Douglas K. Mertz, a well-respected Juneau lawyer specializing in environmental and employment law, as well as Native Alaskan and American Indian legal issues. He, too, saw Joe's lawsuit as a case involving the violation of Joe's constitutional rights and gladly agreed to represent Joe.

Decades earlier, Ruth Bader was developing her understanding of those basic constitutional rights. In elementary and high school, she had already begun to shape her thinking and learning about these principles affecting the lives of all Americans. This process continued as she began her studies at Cornell University.

The free-speech and free-expression issues raised by Joe Frederick's case in 2007 had been in the consciousness of many Americans long before. The 1950s was the era of McCarthyism, named after the Republican U.S. senator Joseph R. McCarthy of Wisconsin. McCarthy spearheaded an unrelenting attack on people whom he labeled traitors because their political or social opinions didn't match his view of acceptable "American values." This was also the period of the rise of the Soviet Union, which defined its government as Communist. At that time, McCarthy and his supporters saw Communism as the ultimate threat to the United States, and the Soviet Union as the ultimate enemy, and they did everything they could to frighten the American people. The tense relationship between the United States and the Soviet Union was referred to as the Cold War.

Concerns about fairness and equality were just below the surface at Cornell University, especially for the women students. Ruth was one of a handful of Jewish women students at Cornell, who all had rooms in a cluster in the women's dorm. "It could have been that whoever arranged for housing wanted us to be comfortable," Ruth said. "Or it could have been that they wanted to set us apart from the others."

Cornell was one of only a few coeducational colleges or universities at the time. Like the others, Cornell treated its female students and male students differently. Very distinct rules governed their behavior. For example, during the school week, the women students had to be in their dorm rooms by ten thirty at night, while the men were free to come and go as they pleased. Women and men had different dress codes: women students had to wear raincoats over their athletic shorts when in public, but young male students could freely walk around in their sports gear.

Aside from the official campus rules, the students themselves had social norms for women's academic performance that were not the same as those for men. The young women could not appear to be too smart or competitive, or they would risk not finding a husband in college. During that period, many women attended college in the hope of finding a suitable match. According to Ruth, "The thing to do was to be a party girl."

Though there was not too much open complaining about these examples of unequal treatment, it has been reported that at Cornell in the early 1950s, as at other universities, graffiti was seen on either library walls or inside bathroom stalls with the cynical admonition: "Study hard, get good grades, get your degree, get married, have three rotten kids, die, and be buried." Ruth Bader did, in fact, study very hard. Her strategy to avoid being considered too brainy: find the most obscure libraries on campus and do her studying there, where her friends wouldn't see her.

Very early in her first year at Cornell, Ruth agreed to go on a blind date with a student who was a sophomore, a year ahead of her. His name was Martin (Marty) Ginsburg. Ruth was seventeen and Marty was eighteen. Although Marty described that first date as "a pleasant but undistinguished evening," he soon discovered that Ruth was special. At the time, Ruth was dating someone at Columbia Law School and Marty had a girlfriend at Smith College, so they settled into a comfortable platonic friendship. They were in some of the same classes; outside of class, they talked about their studies and current events. They went to the movies, played golf, and went out for dinner or drinks on weekends. Marty made it clear in those early days that he was interested in what Ruth was thinking, in what she had to say, and in how she saw the future.

Ruth and Marty complemented each other well. Personally, he was talkative and gregarious, while she was quieter, more reserved. They may have come from differing backgrounds—her father was a struggling, not-very-successful small businessman, while his was a well-to-do department store owner—but it didn't take too long for them to realize that this friendship of theirs was turning into something much more serious.

During their friendship and courtship, the two young people devoted themselves to college activities. Marty was on the varsity golf team. On her own, Ruth was active in Alpha Epsilon Phi, the Jewish sorority on campus, and she was the treasurer of the Women's Vocational Information Committee, a group that organized panel discussions about career opportunities for women. The committee also surveyed the future professional interests of women students for an annual report on jobs available to women college graduates. She also served on the Women's Class Council for her graduation year, 1954.

While Marty majored in chemistry, Ruth Bader chose to major in government. This was a logical choice, given the interest she had shown in the structure and functioning of our political system as far back as eighth grade.

Ruth and her classmates were fortunate to have excellent professors. She took classes taught by leading scholars of literature, history, and constitutional law. Later in her life, as a judge and then a justice, she credited her literature teacher, the world-renowned novelist Vladimir Nabokov, with strengthening her reading and writing skills. "He was a man in love with the sound of words," she said later. "He taught me the importance of choosing the right word and presenting it in the right word order. He changed the way I read, the way I write."

Ruth also studied comparative government and American government and took Milton Konvitz's foundations course, American Ideals. Konvitz was an authority on constitutional and labor law, as well as on civil liberties and human rights. This course, especially, was transformative for many of the eight thousand students who took it over the quarter century Professor Konvitz taught it. It enabled Ruth to appreciate the U.S. Constitution as "a magnificent depository of our ideals, both individual and social." Here she learned intensively about the Bill of Rights, the first ten amendments to the U.S. Constitution, which enumerate a series of areas of human existence that are protected from government interference. Most significant among these as they relate to people's most basic freedoms are the rights listed in the First Amendment to the Constitution. Indeed, they are often referred to as the Five Freedoms: freedom of religion, freedom of speech, freedom of the press, freedom of assembly, and freedom to petition the government. Professor Konvitz was insistent that his students understand and value the importance of the freedoms these ten amendments guaranteed.

Ruth's formal introduction to constitutional law was a course taught by Robert Cushman, a highly regarded specialist in questions of civil liberties. Of all her teachers at Cornell, Professor Cushman may have had the most influence on young Ruth. He certainly built on what Professor Nabokov taught her about writing well. She recalled, "In his gentle way, he suggested that my writing was a bit elaborate. I learned to cut out unnecessary adjectives and make my compositions as spare as I could." This was a skill that would serve her well as a lawyer, a professor, a judge, and a Supreme Court justice, for writing well, clearly, and directly is prized in the legal profession. Justice Ginsburg's advice to anyone writing in the law has always been, "Get it right and keep it tight, without undue digressions or decorations."

Among all her professors, Professor Cushman in particular was crucial to Ruth's professional development. Ruth was already attracted to the intricacies of the law and the shapes and patterns of government, including the relationships among all its parts. The courses she was taking helped her develop a sharp and nuanced understanding of the importance of social and political institutions, their interplay, and how this affected the people being governed.

In her junior year, Ruth started to work as Professor Cushman's research assistant. Now she was learning from him both in the classroom and through the work he assigned her outside. Her research focused on the assault on American civil liberties and freedoms represented by McCarthyism and other antidemocratic forces. In addition to being a highly respected professor, Robert Cushman was one of the leading and most vocal scholars of the decades-long struggle between the government forces

Alpha Epsilon Phi Sorority. Ruth Bader is in the first row, that's standing, third from right, wearing a dark scarf over a light top.

that were trying to make ordinary citizens desperately afraid of the Soviet Union and Americans with progressive or radical political and social ideas. He forcefully condemned the ways in which government agencies were hounding and harassing people merely because they were exercising their constitutional rights.

From Professor Cushman, Ruth learned in depth about the dangers to democracy posed by the institutions established as a result of the "Red Scare" and McCarthyism. These organizations had a shared message: that the Russians, or Soviets, were going to take over the world—and the United States in particular—and enslave its people. Professor Cushman had Ruth, his research assistant, doing research on the House Un-American Activities Committee, known as HUAC. She became increasingly distressed when reading about the inquisitorial investigations that were held by that committee and dozens of others like it across the country. Citizens were being swept up by the so-called witch hunt with no evidence of wrongdoing, in complete contradiction to the democratic system that Ruth and her fellow students were learning about.

One of her responsibilities as Professor Cushman's research assistant was to follow the news closely, tracking government investigations into possible treason or subversion in the entertainment industry. She pored over transcripts of the hearings conducted by HUAC and the Senate Internal Security Subcommittee. In her words, "Professor Cushman wanted me to understand that the United States was straying from its most basic values, that is, the right to think, speak, and write freely without big brother government telling you what's the right way to think or the right way to speak or write."

Questions of fundamental rights such as freedom of speech, of the press, of religion, of association, and of the balancing of those rights with public or government interests were of deep concern at Cornell University during the early 1950s, when Ruth was a student there. Several cases, before and during Ruth's college years, involved professors at Cornell University who had come under fire from certain conservative sectors of the alumni and the board of trustees.

Under the cloud of McCarthyism, a number of speakers were invited who some thought were too subversive to speak on campus, and the university was urged to cancel their invitations. Unlike many other institutions in the country, Cornell University was generally steadfast about respecting the First Amendment rights of its students, faculty, and staff to hear speakers from all sides of the issues being discussed and to form their own opinions.

Professor Marcus Singer, a beloved professor of zoology at Cornell, was called to testify before HUAC in May 1953. He was accused of subversive acts. His case was all over the news during Ruth's senior year. Students, faculty, and staff on the Cornell campus discussed his situation. Many students and alumni, including Ruth and Marty, were outraged by what was happening to him. When Professor Singer appeared before the committee, there were some questions he would not answer. "I am prepared to talk freely about myself," he testified, "but I honestly feel that in honor and conscience I cannot . . . I should not talk about my colleagues and associates." Professor Singer's position was founded on his strong belief in his right to hold and express his own ideas and opinions while not speaking or opining about those of other people. His students and the majority of his colleagues supported his principled response.

Shortly before Ruth's graduation, Professor Singer was cited for contempt because he had refused to answer questions about other people's beliefs and opinions. And six months later, he was indicted—charged with a crime. He was tried, convicted, and sentenced to a suspended four-month sentence and a one-hundred-dollar fine. The university, bowing to pressure from trustees, suspended him from teaching, with pay, for the following three years.

When Marty graduated from Cornell in June 1953, he would be taking his first steps toward training for a career. The young couple knew that it would be important for them to share a profession, to speak the same professional language. In Marty's words, they wanted "to be in the same discipline so there would be something you could talk about, bounce ideas off of, know what each other was doing."

Determining their career path involved something of a process of elimination. In an organized fashion, they considered all the possible professions for which they might both train after graduation. Marty could have prepared to go to medical school, but that was crossed off their list because he would be unable to attend the pre-med chemistry labs required by all medical schools—the class schedule would interfere with his activities on the Cornell golf team. They decided against business school, since the ones they might have gone to were not yet admitting women.

During her first couple of years at Cornell, Ruth Bader had become deeply interested in pursuing a legal career. Now Ruth and Marty determined that law was the best profession for them to pursue together. The subject appealed to Ruth ethically: "That a lawyer could do something that was personally satisfying and at the same time work to preserve the values that have made this country great was an exciting prospect for me."

Marty had always wanted to go to Harvard, so he applied to its law school. Although he would inaccurately describe his academic performance at Cornell as being less than stellar ("I stood very low in my class!"), he was accepted. A year later, Ruth applied and was also accepted. Along with her rich social life and participation in campus activities, Ruth was consistently an exceptionally strong college student ("scary smart," one friend of hers recalled), as she had been throughout her education.

Ruth graduated from Cornell on June 14, 1954, with High Honors in Government, her major, and Distinction in All Subjects. She was a College of Arts and Sciences Marshal at the commencement ceremony; in addition, she was on the dean's list and was elected to Phi Beta Kappa and Phi Kappa Phi, national academic honor societies. She was planning to start her first year at Harvard Law School in the fall of 1954, when Marty would be beginning his second year there.

On December 3, 1953, the *Cornell Daily Sun* had announced the engagement of Ruth Bader and Martin Ginsburg. On June 23, 1954, nine days after Ruth's graduation from Cornell, she and Marty were married. Ruth had earned two important degrees—a bachelor's degree and what she referred to sarcastically as "the most important degree . . . not your B.A. but your M.R.S." In an interview many years later, she would explain, perhaps ironically, that Cornell "was the school for parents who wanted to make sure their girl would find a man. Four guys for every woman. If you came out without a husband, you were hopeless." Marty's mother and father, who had come to be like parents to his fiancée, hosted the wedding ceremony and reception at their home in Rockville, New York, with sixteen invited guests.

Martin David Ginsburg, 1953.

Ruth Bader's Cornell yearbook portrait.

Ruth Bader Ginsburg had learned from professors Cushman and Konvitz that "there were lawyers spending their time trying to repair the wounds that existed in our society. There were lawyers standing up for the people who were called before the committees." As she contemplated her future as a law student and then a lawyer, surely she saw herself championing the kinds of causes she had learned about from her mentors. And surely she maintained the same commitment to the freedoms guaranteed by the Bill of Rights as a Supreme Court justice, who, along with her eight colleagues, considered the First Amendment issues raised by Joe Frederick's case in 2007.

Some time after Joe had graduated from high school and was continuing his education at a college in Texas, the U.S. Court of Appeals for the Ninth Circuit had ruled in his favor. However, the Juneau school board and Principal Morse were not satisfied, and they appealed the Ninth Circuit's decision to the U.S. Supreme Court, which agreed to hear the case.

On March 19, 2007, the court heard oral arguments on the case, *Morse v. Frederick*. The U.S. Supreme Court ruled against Joe Frederick by five votes to four on June 25. It was a demoralizing blow for those who believed that even in a school setting, students' free-speech rights should be protected. The four dissenters in the case were Justices John Paul Stevens, David Souter, Ruth Bader Ginsburg, and Stephen Breyer. The majority opinion was based on several interpretations with which the dissenters took issue.

The majority described the students being permitted to go outside to watch the Olympic relay pass-by as a "school-sponsored event" and as a "field trip." During oral argument, Justice Ginsburg questioned this wording, pointing out that "[the students] were released from school, but they were not required to attend this event and they were not required to stand in front of the school on the opposite side. They weren't monitored by their teachers and there were nonstudents in the crowd. So, it was not like a school assembly."

Further, the majority agreed with the school board that the message on Joe's banner was pro–drug use. The dissenters, including Justice Ginsburg, found that contention laughable, calling it a "nonsense banner" and repeating, "This is a nonsense message, not advocacy." She and her fellow dissenters forcefully maintained that any rule, even in a high school, that permitted only one point of view to be expressed would be an erroneous rule. With the majority decision, students' speech rights suffered a significant setback.

Although Joe Frederick ultimately lost his free-expression battle in the Supreme Court, he knew that among his staunch supporters was Justice Ruth Bader Ginsburg, who had been steadfast in her belief that free speech must be protected vigorously.

FOUR

Marriage Rights, Past and Present

JIM OBERGEFELL WAS a real estate broker in Cincinnati, Ohio. John Arthur was Jim's first significant boyfriend. They met in 1992 and after a couple of dates realized they were serious about each other. Jim's family was supportive of this relationship, but John Arthur's family took a while to get used to the idea that the two young men were in love and planned to spend the rest of their lives together.

For the next twenty years, Jim and John enjoyed a happy and productive life, sharing a home and a business. Then John started falling down more and more often and had increasing difficulty moving. In 2011 he went to the doctor and was diagnosed with ALS (amyotrophic lateral sclerosis), also known as Lou Gehrig's disease.

Over the years, Jim and John had spoken of marriage but had not done anything about it, primarily because Ohio, where they lived, was at that time one of the few remaining states where two people of the same gender were not allowed to wed. They had not wanted to leave their home in order to get married. But when John's illness progressed and it was clear that he would not live much longer, the couple decided to travel to a state where they could legally marry.

They went to Maryland, which did permit same-sex marriages. Because John was so ill by then, they could not drive to Maryland or fly on a commercial plane. Thanks to the generosity of the couple's friends and family, Jim and John were able to fly to Baltimore/Washington International Airport in a medical transport plane. They were married in the plane, on the airport's tarmac, with John's aunt Paulette officiating, and then they immediately flew back to Ohio. "In a perfect world," Jim said, "I could've put John in his wheelchair and taken him six blocks to our county courthouse to get our marriage license and then marry in the comfort and safety of our home. But unfortunately, we didn't have that luxury." Three months after their wedding, in October 2013, John Arthur died. He was forty-eight years old.

Unlike most states, in addition to prohibiting same-gender or same-sex marriages, Ohio did not recognize marriages between two men or two women that had been performed legally in another state or country. This law had real consequences for John and Jim and for thousands of others in similar situations. When John died, because Ohio did not recognize Jim as his widower, Jim did not have the legal standing of a widower in a "traditional" marriage. As the surviving spouse in a legal marriage that Ohio did not recognize, Jim would not be able to receive the Social Security survivor benefits that would have come to him if he had been married to a woman.

Jim had not been expecting this outcome. He had believed that his legal Maryland marriage would be recognized by Ohio authorities and that he would be officially considered John's widower, with all the rights and responsibilities of that status. Earlier that year, the U.S. Supreme Court had ruled in the case *United States v. Windsor* that it was unconstitutional for federal government agencies, such as the Social Security

Administration, to interpret "marriage" and "spouse" as referring only to opposite-sex unions. This decision had strengthened Jim's assumption that his status would be recognized.

But for Jim, and for many others in similar situations, the results of the Supreme Court's decision in *U.S. v. Windsor* would take quite a while to become law throughout the nation, even though what the court rules in such cases is deemed to be the law of the land. Putting Supreme Court decisions into practice in each state faces delays ranging from bureaucratic to purposeful, often in the face of local hostility and resistance. This has historically been the case, for example, with high court rulings strengthening racial equality, as in the school-desegregation and voting-rights cases.

The marriage-equality case decided by the Supreme Court on which Jim Obergefell had pinned his hopes had been brought by Edith "Edie" Windsor. She had been in a committed relationship with Thea Clara Spyer for more than forty years when Thea died in 2009. The two women had lived in New York City. Because at that time they were not able to marry there legally, they had gone to Canada to wed in 2007. In May 2008, a year before Thea's death, the state of New York began recognizing same-sex marriages legally performed in other states and countries.

When Thea died, Edie believed that she would be treated like any other widow. She fully expected that upon inheriting the sizable estate Thea had left her, she would be exempt from paying federal estate taxes on her inheritance—a requirement not applied to a surviving spouse. Edie was outraged when she was treated not as the legitimate survivor of a deceased spouse but as if she and Thea had been roommates or even strangers.

Edie Windsor refused to let this injustice remain unchallenged. She sought and found an attorney willing to help her. Roberta Kaplan was a partner at a prestigious law firm in New York City. Once Roberta heard the details of Edie's situation, she did not hesitate to take the case.

Working closely with attorneys from the ACLU, Roberta Kaplan took Edie's case all the way to the Supreme Court, where she won. On June 26, 2013, a five-to-four decision was handed down by the court. Justice Ruth Bader Ginsburg voted with the majority, holding that the federal government could not treat legally married same-sex partners differently than legally married opposite-sex partners.

Edie Windsor (left) with attorney Roberta Kaplan after their Supreme Court victory.

It was a wonderful and affirming victory for hundreds of thousands of couples, as it meant that *all* federal laws would be applied equally, regardless of the gender of the two spouses. These laws included benefits of all kinds: tax, social security, estate planning, government, employment, medical, death, family, housing, consumer. More than one thousand federal laws had applied only to opposite-sex married couples—laws that gave rights, protections, and benefits to them but not to married same-sex couples. The court's decision in Edie Windsor's case changed all that, requiring that all married couples be treated equally. However, it was one thing for the Supreme Court to issue a ruling and quite another thing for the appropriate officials and authorities in all fifty states and the District of Columbia to change their state and local laws, rules, and practices to reflect the high court's position.

Jim Obergefell and John Arthur had married a month after the decision favoring Edie Windsor. When John died a few months later, Jim believed he would be protected and given those thousand-plus benefits that opposite-sex couples received, including those available to widows and widowers. In fact, the two men had decided to marry legally precisely because they knew that John would die soon, and they wanted to be sure that Jim was protected as his surviving spouse.

Jim realized that his only recourse was to take the matter to court. He made the decision at a good time, since several other, similar cases were being brought around the country. The team of lawyers that was assembled in Jim's case to argue for equal treatment and recognition of same-sex marriages was extremely well versed and well prepared. Mary Bonauto and her colleagues had worked on many similar cases over the years. In fact, since the early 1990s, lawyers like them and women and men around the country had begun to agitate for equal civil rights for lesbians and gays. These rights included the right to marry the person of one's choosing. The movement in support of marriage equality drew tremendous energy from the history of the fight against marriage inequality in the area of racial equality. It had not been until 1967 that a Supreme Court decision, *Loving v. Virginia,* unanimously overturned all state bans on marriages between white people and black people.

In 1953, Marty was in his first year at Harvard Law School and Ruth planned to start there the following year. The newlyweds were preparing for the joint experience of Harvard Law School when Marty was drafted into the U.S. Army.

Their first two years of married life took place on a military base in Oklahoma. Marty had to take a leave of absence from law school, and Ruth had to postpone her plan to enroll there herself as a first-year student. The young couple traveled to Fort Sill, Oklahoma, where Marty became an artillery officer and Ruth got a job as a clerical worker at the local Social Security office.

Ruth and Marty's relationship was tested early in their marriage. Their plans for law school had been put on hold, and they were starting out in an unfamiliar place. And very soon they found out that Ruth was expecting their first child. As they had done at Cornell when they methodically planned their future together, they now put their minds to the situation and worked out approaches to housekeeping and child-rearing that would use their talents and energies and at the same time allow each to support the other.

Sharing a home for the first time, the young couple learned to accommodate and balance each other's strengths and weaknesses. Marty recalled that the first meal Ruth cooked for him was tuna noodle casserole, which

in his words was "as close to inedible as food could be." Instead of making Ruth's poor performance in the kitchen a permanent obstacle to their ability to live together in harmony, Marty taught himself to cook.

They had received a copy of a fancy French cookbook as a wedding gift. It was called *The Escoffier Cookbook,* and many people at the time deemed it the bible of French cuisine. Marty had been a chemistry major in college and approached each recipe as a scientist would, analyzing the ingredients and how they interacted with one another and with other variables such as heat and cooking time. By the end of their two years in Oklahoma, he had cooked his way through the entire book and then some.

Two things happened in Oklahoma that Ruth would recall later as she became a civil-rights attorney. For one, some of her colleagues in the Social Security office overtly discriminated against Native Americans. Oklahoma had the largest Native American population of any state, so it was to be expected that the Social Security office had contact with a great many Native American people. Generally, anyone coming in to apply for Social Security benefits could present any of a number of types of identifying documents. However, the Social Security clerks demanded that Native Americans bring birth certificates when they applied. This, the clerks knew, was a virtually impossible requirement, as that generation of Native Americans had been born during a time when births among their people "were not considered worth documenting." Ruth was horrified by this practice, finding it cruel and unfair. Whenever she could, she assisted Native American applicants and accepted any valid form of ID.

Second, Ruth Bader Ginsburg also experienced a personal encounter with gender discrimination. She had been slated to take a placement exam that would have allowed her to move up a couple of notches at the Social Security office, providing a little increase in both status and pay. But when her supervisor found out she was pregnant, he canceled her exam, telling

Newlyweds Marty and Ruth in Oklahoma.

her that as a pregnant woman, she would not be eligible to travel for the training that would lead to the higher-level position.

This rebuff shook Ruth deeply and raised serious concerns about whether as the mother of a small child she would be able to perform successfully in law school. She worried that she would not be taken seriously, that she would be viewed negatively, because she had a young child. She took her worries to her father-in-law, who had always been supportive and loving. His advice gave Ruth the clear-sightedness to move forward with her plans. If she really wanted to go to law school, having a baby should not deter her. "If you want to be a lawyer," he told her, "you will stop feeling sorry for yourself and you will find a way."

Ruth and Marty's daughter, Jane, was born in Oklahoma on July 21, 1955. Now Ruth fully recognized how fortunate she was that Marty was her husband and Jane's father. The two parents shared all the main parenting activities, with Marty taking the two a.m. feeding. They confirmed that Marty's ever-increasing skills in the kitchen were greater than Ruth's, and from that time on, he was responsible for cooking the family's main meals. The Cornell Chorus, at their alma mater, had scoffed at the fantasy of domesticated husbands in a satirical version of a revered school song, declaring, *"We want to find husbands who cook, clean, and sew, and take care of the children."* Marty was certainly that kind of husband.

This family was a far cry from what Justice Ginsburg, many years later, described as marriage under the common-law tradition, "a relationship of a dominant male to a subordinate female." She had been raised to expect a certain degree of equality between men and women. When she and Marty had talked about spending the rest of their lives together, they were equal partners in the planning process. When they married and had

The Ginsburg family at play, 1958.

a family, they were equal partners in the management of the home and the care of the children.

Theirs was a remarkable marriage in every way. In the 1950s, when they met and married, the concept of the marriage relationship as a union of equals was very rare. Serious public discussion about the need to change social attitudes toward the role of women and toward marriage was just beginning. The movement that would ultimately grow into the second wave of feminism was still a few decades away.

When Ruth and Marty married, they were relatively young: she was twenty-one and he was twenty-two, and they were both still students. From Ruth's perspective, their youth enabled them to develop such an egalitarian relationship. They were both more flexible and less tied to convention than an older couple might have been. She also reported that "Marty was an extraordinary person," that in their marriage "one accommodate[d] the other," and that they were always each other's best friend. They were not the least bit competitive with each other, nor did Marty feel threatened by his highly intelligent partner. "My dear Marty was so comfortable with himself that he never regarded me as being any kind of threat," she recalled. Each of them soon became the rock on which the other could depend. Their marriage was often held up as the kind of relationship to which many aspired, but it was uncommon, requiring a couple willing to practice intellectual and domestic equality.

By the time Jim Obergefell's case reached the U.S. Supreme Court, most lawyers and judges were very familiar with the legal underpinnings of the claim that marriage equality should be an established right.

In particular, the Fourteenth Amendment to the U.S. Constitution stands for the proposition that all citizens deserve fair and equal treatment by officials of local, state, and federal governments. This is referred to as their right to due process: for a government official, office, or agency to deprive someone of a constitutionally guaranteed right, that entity must first allow that person an opportunity to challenge or protest the act, and provide them with a rational explanation of why the government should be permitted to proceed. So, for example, if a person is dismissed from a job with the government, or an individual's property is taken over by an official agency, she is entitled to demand fairness and transparency. In addition, due process includes the right to privacy, which means the right to make personal decisions like whom to marry without interference from the government.

Further, if one category of person can exercise a specific right, then all persons should be able to do the same; they are all entitled to equal protection under the law. This has been the argument behind cases involving voting rights (if white citizens can vote, then citizens of color should be able to), school and housing desegregation (schools and housing should be made equally available to all people, regardless of race), equal pay demands (women should be paid the same as men for equivalent work), and marriage equality, among others.

Justice Ginsburg had always held the firm belief that the Fourteenth Amendment specifically extends constitutional protections to all citizens, regardless of their race, gender, religion, national origin, status, or wealth. Ordinary citizens may challenge actions taken by their government, at any level, that are perceived as detrimental to their rights.

Jim Obergefell's team of lawyers asked the U.S. Supreme Court to answer two questions: Did the Fourteenth Amendment require all states to issue marriage licenses to couples of the same sex? Did this amendment require all states to recognize legal marriages between same-sex couples that took place in another state?

On June 26, 2015, exactly two years after Edie Windsor won her case before the U.S. Supreme Court, this same court majority of five to four resoundingly answered yes to Jim's two questions. Justice Ginsburg and four of her colleagues ruled that not only must the state of Ohio recognize Jim Obergefell as the legal surviving spouse of John Arthur, but also every state in the union and every United States territory now had to make legal marriage available to same-sex couples on the same basis as for opposite-sex couples.

In agreeing with the majority position, Justice Ginsburg expressed the strong commitment to fairness and equality that she had lived in her daily life. Her fifty-six-year marriage to Marty was a strong relationship of equals. She wanted all people to have the opportunity to share in this kind of partnership. And, practicing what she preached, shortly after the decision in *Obergefell,* she went on to become the first Supreme Court justice to officiate at a marriage between partners of the same sex.

FIVE

WOMEN WORKING IN "A MAN'S WORLD"

ILLY McDANIEL WAS born on April 14, 1938, in a rural area of eastern Alabama. Her father was an army mechanic; her mother was a homemaker. The family lived in a house with no electricity or running water. As she was growing up, Lilly worked on her grandfather's farm in Possum Trot, dreaming of a better life for herself. In her words, "I was brought up an only child in a very poor county. It taught me to always look for something better. Improving needs to be what drives people."

Lilly reached for her dreams. She completed high school. In 1956, she married Charles Ledbetter, a local army man who would become a highly decorated veteran, and they raised two children in Jacksonville, Alabama. When the children were still quite young, the couple faced some financial difficulties, so Lilly decided to look for work at the local Goodyear Tire factory. Her husband objected at first, but Lilly insisted that this would be a good thing for the family, and she finally prevailed.

In 1979 Lilly applied for a job as a supervisor at Goodyear Tire, a position that until then had been held only by men. When she heard from the company that the job was hers, Lilly was ecstatic. It was her "dream job."

Lilly experienced bias and sexual harassment by some of her male coworkers, particularly other supervisors. Nonetheless, Lilly persevered because she needed the job. And she was committed to standing her ground and not giving in to prejudice against her and the other women working at the plant.

Being a supervisor suited Lilly very well. She loved organizing and supervising her group. "It's like coaching a softball team with youth," she said. "You've got all your players; you've got the enthusiasm. They know their job and you've got your schedule and you've got your equipment and inventory."

Most of the men on Lilly's team had never before worked for a woman supervisor. It is a great tribute to her that she did so well, receiving positive performance evaluations each year, including a "top performance award" in 1995. The people she supervised came to admire her sense of fairness and her work ethic. They called her Miss Lilly, a name she was proud of: "That showed respect."

Lilly was a loyal Goodyear Tire employee for nineteen years. She was a tremendously hard worker. For most of her time there, she was on the night shift as an area manager and then as a supervisor, working the grueling hours from seven in the evening until seven in the morning. It wasn't easy. She recalled: "By the time I realized how bad the [work] environment was for women, I was in my mid-40s and had many bills to pay. I had no choice but to remain in my job to supplement my husband's income. I worked lots of hours, including overtime."

One day in 1998, shortly before Lilly was planning to retire from Goodyear, she found an anonymous note in her mailbox, a "little torn sheet of paper"—she never did find out who put it there—informing her that during those nineteen years, Lilly was being paid less than all the men doing the same job as she. On the slip of paper was a list showing what every area manager earned. Lilly's name was at the bottom, earning the lowest salary in comparison to the men doing the same job. Doing the math, Lilly determined that she had been earning 40 percent less than her male counterparts. In her words, "I was just humiliated and embarrassed, to say the least, that a major corporation could do me that way."

In 1980, a year after Lilly Ledbetter started her job at Goodyear Tire, President Jimmy Carter appointed Ruth Bader Ginsburg as a federal judge. For the next thirteen years, she served on the U.S. Court of Appeals for the District of Columbia Circuit, the most important court in the nation after the U.S. Supreme Court.

Ruth's path to that first judgeship had not been easy. Many of the obstacles she had faced leading up to this prestigious appointment were different from those faced by Lilly Ledbetter and other women workers like her. Even so, Ruth was exposed to situations in which her gender was viewed as a negative rather than a positive factor.

In 1956, Marty had completed the required two years of military service in Oklahoma, and he, Ruth, and baby Jane returned East. Marty began his second year at Harvard Law School, and Ruth started there as a first-year student. The first year of law school is difficult and challenging for all law students. That was especially true for Ruth, one of only nine women students in a class of approximately five hundred. (There was also only one African American student, a man, in the class.) Ruth has said that she would probably have dropped out if it had not been for Marty's constant support as a husband, as a co-parent, and as a fellow law student. Through both first and second years at Harvard Law School, Ruth flourished and performed exceptionally well. In fact, she finished at the top of her class in her second year.

Ruth Bader Ginsburg has often told the story of the special dinner the dean of Harvard Law School held for the women students in her first-year class. When they had assembled at his home, the dean asked each woman in turn to explain why she was at law school taking a seat that would otherwise have been filled by a man. "I was so embarrassed," Ruth recalled. "The dean had each of the women escorted by a distinguished professor. Mine looked more like God than any man I had ever met. He was also a chain smoker, so we were sharing an ashtray on my lap. When I stood to speak, the cigarette butts fell on the living room floor. But I gave him [the dean] the answer he expected: 'My husband is a second-year law student, and it's important for a woman to understand her husband's work.'"

Marty graduated from Harvard Law School in spring 1958 and was immediately offered a prime position as an associate at a high-status New York City law firm. In order to keep the family together, they decided that Ruth would apply to Columbia Law School in New York City as a "visiting student" for her third year. Generally, the school where the law student completes two out of the three years of study awards the juris doctor ("Doctor of Law") or JD degree. When Ruth told the dean at Harvard Law School that she would be completing her legal education at Columbia Law School, he made it clear that under those circumstances Harvard would not be awarding her its JD. Luckily, Columbia Law School was happy to welcome into its third-year class an extremely talented student who was already building a reputation as a fine legal scholar. She would receive a Columbia Law School JD when she completed her final year of law school.

Columbia had made the right decision. Ruth tied for first place in her class when she graduated in the spring of 1959. She had been the only woman editor of the prestigious *Columbia Law Review* out of twenty-five editors during that year, and she was one of only eleven women in a graduating class of 288 people. Ruth was then twenty-six years old.

After law school, Ruth Bader Ginsburg found herself all too frequently in the position of not being considered for available jobs and then of being paid less than men doing the same job, as Lilly Ledbetter had. Women

Ruth Bader Ginsburg (right, second from top) was one of two women on the sixty-member *Harvard Law Review* Board of Editors.

lawyers in general were often steered toward "soft" cases in the law, for example, those having to do with family issues, rather than the more complex, "masculine" cases concerned with business matters and the like. Mostly, though, women were simply cut out of the employment process for lawyers. "Employers would post interview sign-up sheets headed 'Men Only.' We accepted that as the way things were," Ruth recalled.

In the late 1950s, Ruth's extraordinary abilities were apparently insufficient for the employers of recent law school graduates in New York City, where Ruth was hoping to work. She recalls: "I thought I had done a terrific job at Paul, Weiss, Rifkind, Wharton & Garrison [the law firm where she spent the summer after her second year at Harvard Law School] and I expected them to offer me a job on graduation." When the offer of full-time post-graduation employment was not forthcoming, she had more than an inkling that landing a good law-firm job might be more difficult than she had thought.

Ultimately, though, after some of her law school professors intervened on her behalf, she was hired as law clerk to the trial court judge Edmund Palmieri of the U.S. District Court for the Southern District of New York, a position she held for two years—the standard length of this type of clerkship for recent law graduates—from 1959 to 1961.

The law clerk is a judge's right-hand person. The clerk is there to become totally familiar with all the details of every case that comes before the judge. She or he then prepares the judge for hearings, trials, oral arguments, and conferences with lawyers on both sides of a case and their clients. The law clerk is responsible for the efficient flow of cases through the judge's chambers, which can involve scheduling, writing drafts of judicial opinions, reading the many documents submitted by the parties, researching statutes and cases, and other similar tasks. A great deal of writing is expected of the law clerk, who generally takes a first stab at drafting the

Ruth Bader Ginsburg's Columbia University
Law School yearbook photograph.

judge's response to the submissions received. Judges generally have deep and frequent discussions with the clerk or clerks about the cases before them, seeking fresh views of various legal issues.

Being a law clerk was a perfect job for Ruth Bader Ginsburg. It allowed her to refine her legal research and writing skills. Further, it acquainted her with actual practices inside the specialized world of courts of law, developing proficiencies and having experiences that would serve her well throughout her career.

As Judge Palmieri's law clerk, Ruth labored tirelessly, displaying a work ethic that had been developing since her elementary school years. She arrived in chambers early, stayed late, and continued focusing on her current assignments once she was at home in the evenings and on the weekends. In fact, her performance was so exceptional that the judge, who had been hesitant about hiring a woman as his law clerk, went ahead and hired another woman as Ruth's successor. And Ruth's reputation as a brilliant young lawyer finally brought offers from New York law firms seeking to hire a woman (possibly their first woman) attorney.

But Ruth had other plans. In 1961, she had been approached by Professor Hans Smit, the Dutch-born founder and director of the Columbia Law School Project on International Procedure. He invited her to join the Project in studying Swedish legal procedure and then cowriting a book about the subject. Ruth became his research associate that first year. By the second year, she had been appointed associate director. Doing this work built on Ruth's deep interest in civil procedure. Though as a law student she had studied criminal law, Ruth was always more interested in the rules and practices governing how lawsuits are brought in civil court and how these cases proceed through the courts.

Though most of the work with the Project on International Procedure took place in the United States, Ruth spent several months in Sweden during each of her two years of involvement. During her first visit to Sweden, she learned the language well enough to read and understand Swedish legal treatises on procedural practices. Even years later she could watch Swedish-language films, such as Ingmar Bergman classics, without reading the English subtitles. She and Anders Bruzelius, a Swedish city court judge, wrote and published the projected book; she also coauthored an article on the Swedish legal profession.

Ruth spent four months in Sweden in 1962, where she was joined by

Marty and Jane. Jane was with her again for the several months of her second visit. Those two periods living abroad, mostly with her daughter, were memorable times for the entire family.

The two visits to Sweden enabled Ruth to develop into an expert in a boutique field of law and publish a book under her name. She believed that her experience in Sweden truly opened her eyes to issues of gender discrimination and gender equality. She noticed that about 25 percent of the Swedish law-student population were women, while in the United States women made up only 3 percent of law students—a statistic that spoke volumes.

It was also in Sweden that she read Simone de Beauvoir's book *The Second Sex,* which had been published in France in 1949 and was almost immediately translated into dozens of languages. In this book, the author, a well-known French writer and philosopher, explored the subjugation of women throughout history, casting new light on social, cultural, and political oppression. For many women of the period, *The Second Sex* served as a call to action to end gender inequality.

Ruth was deeply moved by this book. It led her to view from a fresh perspective the situation of women, who were treated as second-class citizens both legally and culturally. For her, de Beauvoir's book "shows the differences between the way women are treated [and] the way men are treated, and it doesn't inevitably have to be that way." This new clarity about gender disparities probably helped Ruth to place in a social and historical context her experiences as a young female college student expected to be pretty but not too smart; as a woman law student expected to justify taking a man's seat in the class; and as a brand-new woman attorney expected to take a lesser job than any male law graduate—no matter what his academic accomplishments—or no legal job at all. And it no doubt helped her see even more clearly the unfairness of the social pressures that kept her brilliant mother from achieving all that her capabilities would have allowed.

Moreover, the manner in which gender issues were frequently and openly discussed by the Swedish people made Ruth think about them in new ways. During her stay there, Ruth recalled, there was a great national debate among the Swedes concerning the need for women to work outside the home in order to provide a second income to the family. But then, when evening came, the women who had worked at full-time paying jobs were expected to cook, clean, and care for the children, while the men could just put their feet up and relax after a hard day at work. Ruth read an article in a Stockholm newspaper by a Swedish woman writer who asked, "Why should the woman have two jobs and the man only one?" Perhaps this caused Ruth to reexamine ideas she had begun developing about gender equity in the United States and to apply some of the lessons she learned in Sweden to the American situation.

Ruth Bader Ginsburg returned to the United States in the fall of 1963 greatly energized by her experiences in Sweden. While pondering how to direct that new energy, she was hired as an assistant professor at Rutgers Law School in Newark, New Jersey. She was one of only two women law professors at Rutgers, and one of a very few throughout the entire country. She was only the nineteenth woman in the United States to be appointed to a law school teaching position with tenure (job security) or tenure track (the possibility of future job security).

Professor Ginsburg worked at Rutgers Law School for nine years, rising to the rank of assistant professor and receiving tenure in 1970. She had been hired to teach civil procedure, the specific rules and standards that govern how civil lawsuits are begun and how they move through the system. Many might find this subject area dry, but Professor Ginsburg was passionate about it. She soon earned the reputation of being an excellent teacher, described by one former student as "very meticulous, very careful, very serious about getting everything right."

This manner of working—painstaking, focused, and virtually perfectionist—was characteristic of her consideration of every professional undertaking. At home, Ruth could often be found still at the dining room table very early in the morning, working on a case, with her favorite snack—a box of dried fruit—at hand. But despite the seriousness of her approach to teaching a subject that didn't excite everyone, one of her former law students recalled, "I loved to hear her think out loud, almost as if she was having a conversation with the author of the text."

The 1960s had seen a steady increase in the number of women applying to and being accepted at law schools throughout the United States. Though there were not large numbers of women law students yet, there were enough at Rutgers Law School to form a significant segment of the student body. In 1970, a group of Professor Ginsburg's women students asked her if she would be interested in teaching a course on gender discrimination and the law. "I repaired to the library," she remembered. "There, in the space of a month, I read every federal decision *ever* published involving women's legal status, and every law review article. That was no grand feat. There were not many decisions and not much in the way of commentary. Probably less altogether than today accumulates in six months' time." Professor Ginsburg designed a seminar: Women's Rights: Sex Discrimination and the Law.

During her Rutgers years, Professor Ginsburg decided to volunteer her professional energies and skills to represent clients in courtroom settings. "I was teaching procedure and I had never worked full-time for a law firm," she said. "The one way I could respectably get litigation experience was to be a volunteer lawyer for the ACLU, the American Civil Liberties Union, which was and is dedicated to supporting people and

Professor Ginsburg, Rutgers Law School.

organizations seeking legal protections for their civil rights and civil liberties." The New Jersey chapter of the ACLU was always looking for such volunteers, and Professor Ginsburg soon had more than enough cases to handle. She was recognized early on as a formidable litigator, successfully arguing cases in court, as well as a strategic negotiator, winning many cases before they reached a courtroom.

At that time, cases involving gender discrimination were almost always given to women attorneys, and Ruth Bader Ginsburg found herself beginning to develop a specialty in that area. She began making connections between the academic subject matter she had studied as a law student and was teaching as a law professor and the on-the-ground legal work that lawyers across the country were doing in the field of gender discrimination.

She was especially interested in a series of cases involving New Jersey public schoolteachers who were forced out of their jobs when they were in the fourth or fifth month of pregnancy. The women were let go without the guarantee of a job—any job—once they wished to return to work. Their plight certainly resonated with Professor Ginsburg, who had faced precisely this type of discrimination in her own life.

During this period, Ruth Bader Ginsburg looked back at her time in Oklahoma as the point when she began to understand that distinctions between what a man could do and what a woman could do were generally socially and culturally constructed, not innate or biological. Her thinking on these matters had evolved over the years, stimulated by her time in Sweden and by her encounters with law students, especially women law students, and other members of her profession. She saw clearly that women were capable of doing virtually anything men could do, given the desire to do so and appropriate preparation.

Meanwhile, Professor Ginsburg continued to make herself available to the ACLU as a volunteer attorney. A case at Rutgers reaffirmed her commitment to changing the imbalance in gender rights over the long term. The undergraduate college at Rutgers was all male. Douglass College, considerably smaller, functioned as the undergraduate women's part of Rutgers. But by the time Professor Ginsburg was teaching at the law school, Rutgers had been designated as the state of New Jersey's public university. Having all-male and all-female colleges affiliated with it would be difficult to sustain, because under the law, public institutions were prohibited from discriminating on the basis of gender.

Professor Ginsburg filed a lawsuit on behalf of one of the gardeners working on the grounds of the campus. His son could attend Rutgers University tuition-free as the son of an employee. His daughter, on the other hand, could attend only Douglass and was unable to secure a tuition waiver because Douglass did not have a waiver program for the daughters of employees.

Professor Ginsburg also took on a case challenging a special summer-in-engineering program run by Princeton University for inner-city sixth graders—only boys were eligible, not girls. And she represented the high school student Abbe Seldin, who in 1972 wanted to join the men's tennis team at her school but was not permitted to do so. Before there was a court ruling in this case, the high school team changed its policies and Abbe was allowed to join the boys, as were all female students who wanted to play tennis.

In 1972, Professor Ginsburg accepted the offer of a teaching position at Columbia Law School, the first woman to be appointed to a tenured position there. At Columbia Law School, Professor Ginsburg continued to teach civil procedure, and she also moved forward in the development of her course on gender discrimination and the law. Because there were no

Professor Ginsburg was the first woman appointed to the faculty, and the first to earn tenure, at Columbia Law School.

casebooks (as textbooks are known in a law school setting) on the subject, Professor Ginsburg and the handful of other law professors around the country who were beginning to teach similar courses had to count on photocopied readings for their students. So, to meet a growing need, Professor Ginsburg, together with two like-minded colleagues from other law schools, published the first such casebook in 1974: *Cases and Materials on Sex-Based Discrimination.*

Throughout the 1970s, the ACLU received many complaints concerning women who worked in local factories and could not obtain family coverage under their health plans, while male workers received coverage for their families. When she was at Rutgers Law School and at Columbia Law School, Professor Ginsburg took on many of these cases, as well as other gender-discrimination cases in which men and women were receiving different treatment. Though most of her clients were women seeking to remedy discriminatory situations, she also represented men who were not able to access certain benefits available only to women. And, most important, in 1972, Ruth Bader Ginsburg co-founded the Women's Rights Project at the ACLU.

Over time, Ruth Bader Ginsburg developed and perfected strategic approaches to the incremental changing of American law as it affected both women and men. She became skilled at identifying the type of legal case that would, at a particular moment, be most likely to succeed, and selected the cases she worked on with this strategy in mind. Along with working on cases that challenged laws or policies that discriminated against women and favored men, her process included a controversial focus on challenging laws or policies that discriminated against men by denying them rights that women enjoyed, from parental leaves for mothers but not for fathers to lower-priced movie tickets for women on "Ladies' Day," with no equivalent for men. At the time, she was criticized for this approach, because some people thought she should be sticking to the fight to get more rights for women and should not be fighting also for more rights for men. But her strategy for pursuing her goals proved to be sound and successful.

In 1998, when Justice Ginsburg had been on the U.S. Supreme Court for five years, Lilly Ledbetter was learning more about the implications of the wage discrimination she had been subjected to during her nineteen years of dedicated work at Goodyear Tire. Lilly realized that her lower pay would forever be reflected in the pension she would receive upon retirement from the company, which would be lower than the pensions male workers received. Though she felt humiliated at first, Lilly soon became angry about the injustice that had been perpetrated against her and all the other female workers at the plant. She decided to pursue a legal route and filed a complaint with the EEOC, the Equal Employment Opportunity Commission, which is the federal government agency that investigates workers' complaints of discrimination by their employers. The EEOC is responsible for enforcing federal laws that make it illegal to discriminate against job applicants or employees because of their race, color, religion, sex/gender, national origin, age, or disability.

Although Lilly's family was skeptical about the likelihood of her winning such a case, they supported her wholeheartedly. They all understood that it would take time—"None of those cases are ever solved overnight." No one in the family anticipated that her case not only would go to the U.S. Supreme Court but also would ultimately result in federal legislation bearing her name.

After following the procedural steps necessary for the type of lawsuit she brought against Goodyear Tire, Lilly found herself almost ten years later facing what must have been one of the biggest disappointments of her life. In 2007, the U.S. Supreme Court voted five to four that Lilly had waited too long to file her complaint against Goodyear Tire. According to federal law, such complaints had to be filed within 180 days after the employer committed the illegal act. Lilly could not have filed a complaint within 180 days of the first time her employer illegally paid her less than her male counterparts, because she was not aware of this discrimination until she had worked at Goodyear for almost nineteen years.

Luckily for Lilly Ledbetter, Justice Ruth Bader Ginsburg, who was writing the dissent in her case, instantly recognized the unfairness of Lilly's situation. She saw what five of her male Supreme Court colleagues did not, could not, see: the inequity of paying women less than men for doing the same job. Nor did they understand that the discrimination included the women workers' not knowing that it was taking place.

What bothered Justice Ginsburg was how narrowly the Supreme

Court majority of five justices looked at Lilly's case. They thought that within 180 days after the first time the company paid her less, Lilly should have been able to figure out that she was being paid less than men doing the same supervisory work. In other words, she lost because for a long time she did not know she was being discriminated against. Justice Ginsburg, at that time the only woman sitting on the Supreme Court, strongly believed that the Lilly Ledbetter case "was one that every woman understood, but my colleagues, unfortunately, didn't."

As Justice Ginsburg pointed out in her scathing dissent, most, if not all, employees do not know what others are being paid for doing the same job. Most employers will not share that information, particularly private companies like Goodyear Tire. In fact, when Lilly started at that company, she was instructed specifically not to discuss salaries with anyone at all, with the strong implication that if she violated that policy, she could be fired.

The Lilly Ledbetter story did not end with the court's decision. As sometimes happens when a minority opinion points out a flaw in a federal law, Justice Ginsburg's dissent served as a signal to Congress that a statute needed to be rewritten or corrected. Although Lilly lost her appeal in the Supreme Court, Justice Ginsburg's sharp and detailed dissent led the United States Congress to recognize the unfairness of setting a 180-day time limit for reporting a case of pay discrimination at work.

The Lilly Ledbetter Fair Pay Act was passed in the U.S. Senate by a vote of sixty-one in favor to thirty-six against. There had been widespread public support for such a law, and citizens organized nationwide to let Congress know that people of all political persuasions condemned the court's narrow interpretation as unjust. On January 29, 2009, President Barack Obama signed the bill into law as his first act in office. That law ensures that if a worker experiences discriminatory acts based on race, gender, age, or the other specified categories, and those acts occur over time, the affected worker has 180 days to file a complaint after she or he *learns* of the discriminatory act.

Together, Lilly Ledbetter and Justice Ruth Bader Ginsburg moved American law a little further in the direction of protecting all people from discrimination at work. Both of them understood that there are times when a woman's experience of the world is simply different from a man's, and that it is important to open male eyes to those female experiences. In Justice Ginsburg's words, "Ledbetter was a wonderful example of how a defeat can be turned into a victory."

Lilly Ledbetter (right), with First Lady Michelle Obama, at President Obama's signing of the Lilly Ledbetter Fair Pay Act.

SIX

PROTECTING ALL CAREGIVERS

I N 1958, CHARLES E. MORITZ, who lived in Denver, Colorado, realized that his elderly mother was in failing health and needed to move out of her home, where she was living alone, and move in with him. Charles was a lifelong bachelor who worked as the western editor for Lea & Febiger, a publishing company based in Philadelphia, Pennsylvania. The job required him to travel a great deal in order to check in with authors in eleven western states. He also had to make almost daily visits to Colorado schools of medicine, dentistry, and veterinary medicine, and to attend conventions and gatherings of life-science professionals throughout the United States.

For a few years, his mother did well during his absences, and Charles was happy to provide more than half her financial support and his companionship when he was home. Eventually, though, Mrs. Moritz's arthritis worsened, and in 1963 she was confined to a wheelchair. At the same time, she was beginning to exhibit memory loss, deafness, and other signs of aging. It was clear to Charles that his mother was both physically and mentally unable to care for herself any longer.

Charles hired Cleeta Stewart as a housekeeper who would also serve as a caregiver for his mother. In 1968, after several years of paying the housekeeper's wages, Charles realized that the income-tax law allowed a deduction for home-care costs in caring for elderly parents. So, that year, when he prepared his income-tax returns, Charles took a six-hundred-dollar deduction, reducing the amount of tax he owed the federal government.

Some months later, Charles received a distressing letter from the Internal Revenue Service, or IRS. This is the federal agency responsible for collecting taxes and supervising the implementation of the laws and rules in the Internal Revenue Code. The IRS informed Charles that he was not eligible for the home-care deduction, which was allowed only for women (single, married, divorced, or widowed) or for men who were married or had been married. In other words, since Charles was a man who had never been married, he could not receive a tax benefit for caring for his elderly mother. Though he was not a lawyer, Charles believed that he was receiving unfair, unequal treatment because he was not a married or formerly married man or an unmarried woman. One group of people, to its detriment, was being treated differently from other groups.

Charles appealed the Internal Revenue Service's initial decision, but his claim was denied once again. He investigated his options and determined that he would have to appeal to the United States Tax Court. Charles decided that the matter was so clear-cut—that the way the rule was being applied was so obviously unfair—that he would be able to make a good case on his own before that court. Charles appealed the decision of the Internal Revenue Service, appearing *pro se* ("for himself"), without a lawyer.

Surely, Charles thought, anyone would have seen that the distinction made "no sense," as he said in his written brief to the tax court. How could it be fair that the so-called babysitter deduction was available for any adult except a man who had never been married? Why could any woman take a tax deduction for taking care of her elderly parent, while a never-married man like Charles Moritz could not?

The tax court disagreed with Charles. But Charles didn't know that all tax-court decisions are published as "advance sheets," made available to lawyers by the court before the official court decision is published in a bound volume. This meant that the tax court's decision against him was widely read by tax attorneys nationwide.

While Ruth was teaching Civil Procedure and Constitutional Law at Rutgers Law School and representing clients through the New Jersey chapter of the ACLU, Marty, at that time working at a major law firm in New York City, was one of the country's most prominent tax attorneys.

Marty and Ruth always brought work home with them in the evenings, and they had set up small work spaces in two different rooms in their New York City apartment. One evening in the fall of 1970, while they were in their separate work areas, Marty read the advance sheets of the case that Charles Moritz had lost before the tax court and realized immediately that he and Ruth might be able to work on this case together: he knew the tax code inside and out, and she knew the U.S. Constitution inside and out.

As Marty would later relate, "I went next door, handed the advance sheets to my wife, and said, 'Read this.' Ruth replied with a warm and friendly snarl, 'I don't read tax cases.' I said, 'Read this one,' and returned to my room. No more than 5 minutes later—it was a short opinion—Ruth stepped into my room and, with the broadest smile you can imagine, said, 'Let's take it.' And we did."

Charles Moritz first met his new attorneys in the fall of 1971, when Ruth and Marty flew to Denver from New York to confer with him on the night before they were to argue his case before the Tenth Circuit Court of Appeals. They appeared on behalf of Charles on October 28, 1971. Almost a year later, they learned that they had won the case. Ruth Bader Ginsburg's oral argument in Charles's case was her first at that level of court, heading up a long line of major oral arguments she would deliver over the course of her work as a litigator. Most of these arguments would result in wins for her clients.

On November 22, 1972, in Denver, Colorado, Charles savored what for him must have been a tremendous moral victory when he learned that his lawsuit against the Internal Revenue Service had been won for him by two attorneys whom he barely knew. He had believed all along that justice was on his side, but when he had tried to pursue it on his own, he had been unsuccessful. Luckily for him, though he had lost his case in tax court, Ruth Bader Ginsburg and her husband, Martin Ginsburg, had found the case important enough for them to travel all the way from New York City to represent him free of charge. And they did such a good job that Charles Moritz won the case, not only for himself but for all men who might find themselves in a similar situation.

Ruth Bader Ginsburg was the perfect person to become the legal champion of someone like Charles Moritz. She knew from her own experience that family members of both genders were often called upon to care for a dependent or an ill or dying relative. When her own mother was diagnosed with cancer, Ruth and her father, Nathan, cared for her with love and devotion. And as an adult, Ruth had lived through a hard time as the caregiver of an extremely sick family member.

In 1957, when Marty was in his third and final year at Harvard Law School and Ruth was in her second year, he was diagnosed with testicular cancer. He and Ruth worked through the complications of dealing with Marty's two surgeries, combining his daily radiation treatments—and his sickness following each of them—with caring for two-year-old Jane, and with Ruth's classes. For most of the semester, Marty was too ill to go to class. Ruth would recall: "His classmates, my classmates rallied around the two of us and prepared individual tutorials to help prepare him for exams."

Through Marty's illness, Ruth was there for him, typing his law school assignments and coordinating with his classmates for the delivery of class notes. She also continued to excel in her own studies, maintaining an academic average that was high enough to earn her a coveted position, in her second year, on the *Harvard Law Review*; she was an editor for volume 71 (1957–58) of that revered journal. She was one of two women out of a total of fifty editors. The couple were fortunate that Ruth, over the years, had developed the ability to perform at a high level on very little sleep. "Because of the radiation," she recalled, "Marty couldn't ingest anything until midnight. And so, between midnight and two he had dinner, my bad hamburger usually. And then he would dictate to me his senior paper, and then he'd go back to sleep. And it was about 2:00 when I'd take out the books and start reading what I needed to read to be prepared for classes the next day."

Despite this difficult situation at home, Ruth did exceptionally well in law school that year. Marty, though he had been well enough to attend classes for only two weeks of his final semester, graduated not only on time but *magna cum laude* (with very high honors), thanks to all the support he had received from Ruth and from his classmates, as well as his own fierce determination to survive, flourish, and succeed. Though Ruth could have taken a leave from law school to care for him, she and Marty decided that it would be better for her to stay in school and finish on time. She said later, "Frankly we didn't know how long Marty was going to live, and I might end up being the sole supporter of Jane."

Ultimately Marty recovered from the cancer. For the next five years, they and Marty's doctors were vigilant in checking that the cancer had not returned, and it never did. But the experience of sharing the terrible burden of his illness and of relying on Ruth's abilities to be simultaneously wife, mother, law student, and caregiver gave the two of them a special insight into Charles Moritz's situation.

Though Charles Moritz was able to celebrate his courtroom victory in 1972, he did not live long enough to know how significant it would become in the broader legal struggle for gender equality. In fact, another landmark case had already been developing for five months. In New Jersey, another man's family situation was about to set in motion a series of events that would lead to yet another legal vindication of men's and women's equal rights.

On Monday, June 5, 1972, Stephen Wiesenfeld's beloved wife, Paula, died giving birth to their son, Jason. Stephen was deeply committed to raising Jason as a single, widowed father. In the 1970s, a male parental caregiver and a stay-at-home dad were unusual, and men who assumed these roles were often objects of ridicule. Across the United States, laws, policies, beliefs, and practices were built on the view that women were supposed to keep the home and raise the children while men were responsible for supporting their families by working and "bringing home the bacon."

The Social Security Act was created in 1935 to protect working people by establishing their right to a pension in old age and insurance during unemployment. Like the United States tax code, it was full of rules and regulations that reflected this narrow view of women's and men's roles in society. Stephen discovered that certain benefits were not available to him. As a husband and widowed father, he was not eligible to receive the death benefits to which a widowed wife and mother would be entitled. Throughout their marriage, Paula had been the main breadwinner in the family. Each month she had faithfully contributed to Social Security the maximum allowable amount from her pay as a New Jersey schoolteacher. Even so, after she died, Stephen would not receive any benefit under the Social Security Act that would make it possible for him to raise his son himself. If he had died instead of Paula, as his widow she would have been eligible to receive those benefits. It didn't seem fair to him, and it didn't seem fair to Ruth Bader Ginsburg.

Ruth knew from her own experience that the nurturing of children by their father was not only good and desirable but also critical to the happiness and well-being of both child and father. She also knew that a man could be an actively engaged parent. Her own father had been a traditionalist in many ways. Even so, when Celia became increasingly ill and bedridden, Nathan took on the bulk of the parenting responsibilities for his teenage daughter. In Ruth's adult life, Marty was in all ways the co-parent of their two children, Jane and James. And so, in the early 1970s, when she learned the details of Stephen Wiesenfeld's situation, both Ruth the lawyer and Ruth the wife and mother jumped at the chance to fight for the rights of all parents to care for their children and of all children to receive the most nurturing care possible from a parent. Ruth's "dream for society" had always been "fathers loving and caring for and helping to raise their kids."

The Wiesenfeld case would become a critical legal victory, not just for Stephen Wiesenfeld and for Ruth Bader Ginsburg but for all Americans. In preparing for it, the professor and attorney was strategic at every stage of the lawsuit she filed on Stephen's behalf. This lawsuit, *Weinberger v. Wiesenfeld,* culminated in 1975 with the U.S. Supreme Court's unanimous decision in favor of Stephen Wiesenfeld. This decision immediately invalidated the section of the Social Security Act that excluded men in Stephen's situation from receiving death benefits following the death of their wives. The victory made it possible for Stephen to do what he and Paula had always planned: to be the stay-at-home dad who would care for and raise their child. Stephen and little Jason moved to Florida, where father and son established their home together.

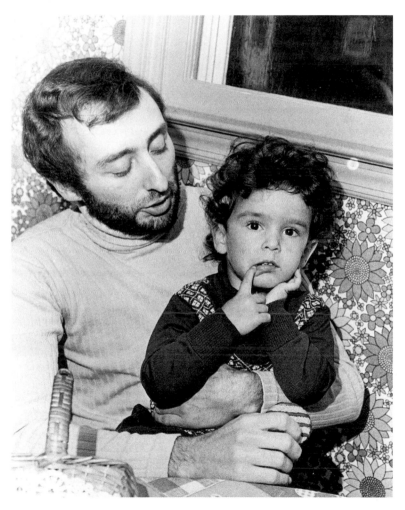

Stephen Wiesenfeld with Jason.

The client-attorney relationship between Stephen Wiesenfeld and Ruth Bader Ginsburg developed into a friendship, beginning around Christmas 1972. The friendship included everyone in the two families: Stephen and Jason; Ruth and Marty and their children. Their connection, both personal and professional, lasted through the years. As she became first a judge and then a justice, Ruth stayed in touch with the Wiesenfeld family. When Judge Ginsburg was nominated to the U.S. Supreme Court in 1993, Stephen Wiesenfeld testified before the United States Congress at the hearings. In his opening words, he described his relationship with his late wife, Paula, by observing, "Not unlike Martin Ginsburg and his wife, Ruth Bader Ginsburg, we were among the pioneers of alternative family lifestyles."

Stephen and Ruth frequently exchanged letters, and the justice sent cards and gifts on special occasions, including Jason's bar mitzvah. She was delighted when, in 1995, Jason chose to go to law school—and not to just any law school, but to Columbia Law School, her alma mater. Incidentally, when she was Professor Ginsburg, she had been teaching at Columbia while she prepared Stephen Wiesenfeld's case in the early 1970s.

Justice Ginsburg officiated at Jason Wiesenfeld's wedding in 1998 and, in 2014, at the wedding of Stephen Wiesenfeld and Elaine Harris. After almost forty years as a single widower, Stephen met the woman whom Justice Ginsburg referred to as "the second love of his life." The justice married them in the beautiful East Conference Room of the U.S. Supreme Court Building.

Ruth Bader Ginsburg's growing-up years gave her a deep respect and love for the institution of family. She carried these feelings with her as she grew and established her own family, then watched her children do the same. Much of the work she was doing as an ACLU attorney while her children were growing up was based on that deep valuing of the family

Justice Ginsburg with Jason Wiesenfeld, about to officiate at his wedding.

unit and the ways family members look out for one another. In undertaking the legal representation of people like Charles Moritz and Stephen Wiesenfeld, Ruth Bader Ginsburg was fighting for fairness, gender equality, and acknowledgment of nontraditional families.

SEVEN

Strengthening the Family Unit

MELISSA LUMPKIN WAS like many young women of her generation. Born into poverty around 1970 to a sawmill worker and a factory hand in rural Mississippi, she did not have a very bright future ahead of her, and the course of her life was somewhat aimless. When Melissa was fifteen, she met young Sammy Lee James, and when she became pregnant, the two married. It was 1985.

Sammy started a business as a cabinetmaker, and Melissa stayed home with first one baby, Samuel, and then, two years later, a second child, Leann. Melissa was still a teenager, and the burdens of motherhood weighed on her. Sammy would work late most nights, and Melissa took to going out with her old friends while her sister watched the kids. Years later, Melissa would say regretfully, "I got mixed up with the wrong crowd."

One of the friends Melissa spent time with was Junior Brooks, whom she had known since childhood. In June 1992, after eight years of marriage, Melissa divorced Sammy and married Junior. Three months later, Sammy also remarried.

Melissa's second husband was not a good provider. He had a criminal record and few employment options. Later statements made in court indicated that he was a serious alcoholic and was physically abusive to

Melissa. Melissa couldn't find stable employment either, working at low-paying jobs like waitressing when she could find them.

For these reasons, Melissa agreed with ex-husband Sammy that the children, Leann and Samuel, would be better off living with him in the relatively nice home he had inherited from his father. She could not afford to consult a lawyer. Without fully understanding what she was doing, she agreed that in exchange for visits with her children, she would pay Sammy forty dollars a week in child support and cover half of the children's medical expenses. Based on what she was earning, it would very soon become impossible for Melissa to keep this agreement.

Sammy claimed that Melissa never came to visit with the children. Melissa said that Sammy and his new wife would not let her spend time with her own two children. Sammy claimed that Melissa never paid him anything toward the agreed-on child support; Melissa asserted that she gave him five hundred dollars in cash and jewelry, and he still would not let her visit the children.

The troubles between the ex-spouses culminated when Sammy went to court in mid-November 1993. He asked that Melissa's parental rights be terminated so that his new wife could adopt the children and raise them as her own. A parental-termination decree is a legal determination by a judge that a parent is unfit to continue playing that role in her or his child's life, and that from that day forward, the person is no longer legally that child's mother or father.

Sadly for Melissa, in 1994 the court sided with Sammy and terminated her parental rights to Leann and Samuel, who were then legally adopted by Sammy's wife. Melissa was not happy with this outcome and finally found an attorney who would try to help her get the trial court's decision reversed by appealing it to a higher court.

While Melissa Brooks was struggling through the labyrinth that was the Mississippi state judicial system, another woman was just beginning to learn the intricacies of serving as a justice on the highest court in the land, the U.S. Supreme Court. Despite their dissimilar backgrounds and life stories, Melissa Brooks and Ruth Bader Ginsburg had a common bond well before their paths crossed. Each of them was moved to act by feelings about her relationship with family, specifically the mother-child relationship.

Ruth's relationship with Marty was very different from that of her own parents, and the couples were from two distinct generations. But they shared an abiding sense of loyalty toward and support of each other and of their children. Ruth's mother was the strongest influence in her young life, providing the guidance and foundation for the powerful intellect that Ruth would develop. Throughout Celia's lengthy illness, Ruth's father worked tirelessly to ensure that his wife and daughter had everything they needed to live as well as possible. He made sure that Celia was comfortable, even as she was slowly succumbing to the cancer that ultimately killed her. And he made certain that Ruth would develop normally as a bright, engaged, and active teenager by making it possible for her to study hard and to participate in the nonacademic activities that made her so well-rounded.

Ruth and Marty's emphasis on family as central to a happy existence led them to keep their family together when they might have lived separately, when Marty was hired by a New York law firm and Ruth needed to complete her final year at Harvard Law School in Cambridge, Massachusetts. Their feelings about family contributed to their commitment to shared parenting while each parent was also engaged in demanding professional responsibilities.

Ruth Bader Ginsburg often remarked that having a child while studying or working full-time was actually a positive thing. During her last year of law school, for example, she was able to balance her schoolwork with her parenting responsibilities in ways that grounded her in both worlds: law school and home. Fortunate to have the help of babysitters who cared for Jane while she and Marty were at school or at work, Ruth could focus exclusively on her studies during the hours she was at school and shift her entire focus to being a mother during the afternoon and evening hours when she was at home with Jane. Putting her daughter to bed, though, was not the end of Ruth's law-student responsibilities for the day. "By the time [Jane] went to sleep for the night, earlier than most children," she remembered, "I was glad to get back to the books."

Sometimes, of course, the nicely balanced life of a student mother could be destabilized by the unexpected realities of living with a young child. Once, when Ruth and Marty were in law school and Ruth was at home, focusing on her studies, the baby found some mothballs, and Ruth discovered her eating them. "We dashed her to Cambridge City Hospital, where her stomach was pumped," she said later. "I recall her screams to this day." The incident reminded Jane's parents all too poignantly that balance and focus needed to be present together at all times.

By the time Jane was in grade school, she had realized that her family was different from the families of most of her classmates. Hers was atypical: both parents worked, and both parents took care of Jane. And, unlike most of her friends' families, in some areas her parents seemed to switch roles. Jane would laughingly say in later years, "Mommy does the thinking and Daddy does the cooking." In the late 1950s, most women were stay-at-home mothers, while men were the breadwinners. "I remember a friend of mine telling me," Jane recalled, "that her mother said she 'had to be nice to [me] because [my] mommy worked.' Like I had leprosy or something."

In the Ginsburg home, Marty was generally the disciplinarian. But Ruth was by no means a softy with her daughter, who later described her mother as "somewhat austere." Jane went on to say, "When I did something bad, which happened often, my dad would yell, but my mother would be real quiet and I'd know she was very disappointed in me." Jane frequently broke family rules; for example, even though candy was strictly forbidden, she would often buy some after school and then lie about it. But her parents always found out somehow, and Jane's misbehavior would be the topic of dinnertime conversation, which otherwise would most likely be focused on some legal matter, in particular, on specific issues that arose in the cases Ruth was handling at the time as an attorney for the ACLU.

Thanks to her mother, Jane learned to read when she was very young. She practiced her reading skills early on by proofreading Ruth's legal papers. Jane often accompanied her mother to the office and the courtroom. Ruth oversaw Jane's homework, requiring her daughter to produce several drafts of any written assignment she was preparing for school and reviewing the finished task.

But Jane's life was certainly not all work and no play. When she was still a baby, her parents had always made sure to have beautiful music playing at feeding time. This practice apparently worked well, and Jane continued to love music as an older child and an adult. As a young child, she went with her mother to as many children's theatrical and musical events as they could fit in on the weekends. Often, when they knew well ahead of time what opera they would be attending on a future weekend, Ruth would play a recording of the piece a long time before the actual performance. If she could find the opera's libretto, or script, she would go over it with Jane to familiarize her with the lines she would be hearing from the stage.

Looking back at her childhood, Jane said, "I never thought I couldn't do anything because I was a girl and I never felt I missed anything because my mother worked." As an adult, Jane became an attorney and a law professor, as her mother had. She marveled at all the things Ruth had been

Ruth and Jane, 1958.

Ruth and Jane, 1965.

able to give her while working as hard as she did in her professional life. "For instance," Jane said, "when I went to sleep-away camp, she wrote regularly. She just sort of has this way of being meticulous and attending to detail that in a way is quite daunting to even think about keeping up with."

Jane was ten years old when she was joined by baby brother James in September 1965. At that time, Ruth was thirty-two years old and on the faculty at Rutgers Law School. When Ruth found out she was pregnant, she was concerned that her teaching contract would not be renewed. She remembered clearly what had happened to her in Oklahoma, when her supervisor at the Social Security office had learned of her pregnancy and denied her a promotion. In those days, it was a widespread practice for employers of all types to place pregnant workers on an indefinite involuntary, unpaid leave, with no guarantee that their jobs would be waiting for them later. To avoid the possibility of this kind of forced leave, Professor Ginsburg wore her mother-in-law's clothes, which were a size larger than she normally wore, and successfully hid her pregnancy. Once she had her signed contract, she made the news of her pregnancy public to her friends and colleagues.

James grew up much as Jane had, with two hard-working parents who managed to give him all the attention a growing child required. He recalled, "The family was always home for dinner," and he experienced Ruth's demanding oversight of his homework each night, as Jane had. James, too, grew up hearing music at home. Although he was described as

James, with a friend, on his fourth birthday.

hyperactive by his teachers (and as "lively" by his mother), at concerts James would listen, totally engaged, "even when he was kindergarten age." It was not surprising, then, that as an adult, after one year in law school, James decided to leave the study of law and devote his life to music. He eventually became the founder of Cedille Records, a not-for-profit record label that produced recordings of classical music.

James's liveliness meant that he was curious and often ignored the family rules, as Jane had. In an episode that seemed to mirror his sister's exploration of mothballs, when James was two and a half and in the care of his nanny, he was crawling around the kitchen, investigating everything. Inside a cupboard, he found an interesting-looking liquid and drank some of it. It was a very toxic chemical drain de-clogger. James was rushed to the hospital. "When we first saw James," recalled his mother, "we were stunned. Deep burns distorted his face, charred lips encircled his mouth— a tiny, burnt-out cavern, ravaged by the lye." But James survived, and the doctors were able to restructure his face so that no visible scars remained.

James also misbehaved as an older child, getting involved in activities his mother called "pranks." One of these so-called pranks happened at his elementary school. On a dare from classmates, James took a group of kindergartners up to the top floor of the building in the hand-operated elevator, which had been momentarily left empty by the elevator operator. Although no one was injured during this elevator joy ride, James did get into trouble with the school principal.

James was extremely talkative, so much so that his family called him Motormouth. He remembered playing a lot of Scrabble with his mother and taking walks with her, during which she would give him complicated math problems to solve in his head. And like his sister, James remembered how hard his mother worked all the time: she was "a night owl who worked into the wee hours after putting her family to bed." His mother's hard work, however, did not mean that she ignored him. As James described it, "She was always there when I wanted her to be—and even when I didn't."

Although they were ten years apart, James and Jane did a lot of their growing up together. Since both parents worked long hours, Jane was often James's appointed babysitter. This wasn't a chore but rather something she enjoyed. In fact, she parlayed her caretaking of James on Sunday mornings, when her parents were getting their much-needed extra sleep, into a valid excuse for her to stop going to Sunday school sessions at a local synagogue.

The Ginsburgs, however, always balanced hard work with relaxation and entertainment. When Jane and James were growing up, the family went on frequent trips within the United States and abroad. Though both parents always took work with them, they did not let that distract them from enjoying adventures and new places as a family. Later on, when their children started their own families, Ruth and Marty were happy to take

The Ginsburgs on vacation in the Virgin Islands, 1980.

on the role of engaged grandparents to their four grandchildren. Years later, when she was a recent law school graduate, Clara Spera remembered fondly the Jewish holiday celebrations she spent with her Bubbie, as she called her grandmother, and the laughter they shared at a performance of the musical *The Book of Mormon*.

Melissa Brooks was not privileged with the background, education, family loyalties, or connections that characterized Ruth Bader Ginsburg's life. She was essentially doomed to a hardscrabble existence that, sadly for her, had included the termination of her parental rights. She would not see her children again, ever, unless she was able to persuade a court that she deserved the right to appeal the harsh decision that took the kids away from her, and to show that she could be a good mother.

Melissa found a local Mississippi lawyer, Robert McDuff, who agreed to take her case *pro bono publico* ("for the public good"), shortened to *pro bono* and meaning that he would represent her for free. Robert McDuff specialized in cases involving poor people and was referred to as "Atticus Finch with a laptop." (Atticus Finch was the fictional Alabama lawyer in the novel *To Kill a Mockingbird*, who represented clients no one else would take on.) Robert McDuff described his philosophy of lawyering as follows: "If it's something that interests me and I think is important—and if I can make a difference—I'll take it on." Clearly, he thought Melissa's situation warranted his assistance.

Even though our legal system is supposed to serve everyone equally whether the person has money or not, in reality most legal proceedings are expensive. Melissa and her attorney could not just go into the court and complain that the decision to take away her children was unfair. First, they would have to pay upfront to provide the required documentation for the argument they were going to present. This would involve both court fees and costs.

In this instance, Melissa was supposed to pay two dollars a page to copy more than a thousand pages of the record of the court hearings that had ended in her children being taken from her. This record included transcripts of everything that was said about the case in the courtroom, the testimony of all witnesses for both sides, and other supporting documents. Melissa was also supposed to pay several hundred dollars more for incidentals such as filing fees, court-reporter charges, and transcripts. Since she was earning only $2.15 an hour plus tips as a waitress, it would have been impossible for her to pay that much. But the rules were clear: If you don't pay, you can't appeal.

Melissa and her lawyer went to the highest state court, the Supreme Court of Mississippi, and asked the court to declare her a pauper, a very poor person, so that she could appeal the court's decision *in forma pauperis*, "as a poor person." If she succeeded, she would be able to appeal without paying court fees or costs.

But that state court denied her request. Melissa would not be able to appeal the loss of her children unless she paid the several thousand dollars of court fees and costs first. She could not do so. But because she was not deemed too poor to pay the court costs, the Mississippi court dismissed her original appeal of the decision to terminate her parental rights.

Only one possibility remained. Robert McDuff submitted a request to the U.S. Supreme Court that it grant *certiorari,* or permission, and hear an appeal of the negative decision by the Mississippi Supreme Court. One of the bases on which the U.S. Supreme Court grants petitions for *cert.,* as they are often called, is if the justices are being asked to review a state court decision that is being challenged as unconstitutional. And the U.S.

Supreme Court agreed to review the decision by the Mississippi Supreme Court in Melissa's case, *M.L.B. v. S.L.J.* (In cases involving custody battles or termination of parental rights, the parties' initials are used rather than their full names in order to preserve their privacy.)

Robert McDuff knew he had a steep hill to climb. There was a good chance that a majority of the nine Supreme Court justices would not see things his way. He expected them to share a concern that if Melissa's situation of poverty was considered sufficient for her to be permitted to appeal the decision against her, then all poor people would think they were entitled to the same benefit, even in cases that were less significant than the loss of parental rights.

At oral argument before the Supreme Court, Robert McDuff focused on the human aspect of his case, the deeply troubling situation of his client Melissa Brooks. He started off with a powerful statement: "My client is no longer the mother of her children in the eyes of the law. The only way she can become their mother again under the law is through the appeal that is available as a matter of right under Mississippi law."

As in almost all oral arguments before the U.S. Supreme Court, there were a great many questions and interruptions by the justices. Looking back at the oral argument on that day, one may infer from Justice Ginsburg's questions and comments her view that it had been wrong to punish Melissa Brooks so severely just because she was poor. In responding to a point that had been made by the attorney for the state of Mississippi, Melissa's opponent, Justice Ginsburg said almost angrily: "This isn't about money." Forcefully she explained that if you lose this kind of case, the end result is that "you are a stranger to the child you bore. That isn't about money."

As it turned out, Justice Ginsburg was indeed on Melissa's side. On December 16, 1996, the justice announced the majority decision from the bench. She summarized the issue: "This case concerns a poor person's opportunity to challenge on appeal a court decree ending her status as a parent." And then she held, for the majority, that "Mississippi may not deny M.L.B. because of her poverty, her inability to pay for a transcript, access to appellate review [of the] evidence on which she was judged unfit to remain a parent."

Although this decision by no means guaranteed that Melissa Brooks would have her parental rights restored, at least it meant that she could go back to court in Mississippi and try to get that decision reversed. After hearing the ruling, Melissa declared: "This is a grand Christmas present. This is the best news I've heard in a long time."

EIGHT

DEFENDING HARD-WON CIVIL RIGHTS

I N THE EARLY 1980s, Inez Wright was a proud resident of Memphis, Tennessee. She had four children in public school: Oscar Clay Renfro, Anthony Lee Renfro, Lisa Marie Wright, and Ephron Antoni Wright. Inez Wright and many other black families in Memphis and elsewhere were becoming increasingly dismayed by the continued existence of segregation in the region's public schools. This was not *de jure* segregation, meaning segregation either ordered by or approved by law, but *de facto* segregation, meaning that although there were laws against separating black and white students into different schools, the schools were in fact not racially integrated. This was happening not just in Memphis but in school systems around the United States.

In 1954, almost thirty years earlier, the U.S. Supreme Court had ruled, in the landmark case *Brown v. Board of Education,* that public schools had to be equally accessible to both black and white children, ending almost a century of segregated school systems nationwide. There was a great deal of resistance to this decision, especially in the southern states and also in some places in the North, such as Boston and New York City.

One of the ways some people defied the Supreme Court's order to integrate schools was by creating segregated private schools, known popularly as "seg academies." These schools, often church-affiliated, were established specifically to appeal to white parents who did not want their children attending school with children of other races. Through a variety of stealth maneuvers and policies—the location of the schools, the cost of tuition, subtle or overtly unwelcoming language in the schools' promotional materials—these private schools made themselves unattractive or inaccessible to most black students and other students of color.

One significant advantage the seg academies (and indeed all private schools) relied on was that they could, at that time, claim tax exemption under the U.S. tax code. These schools paid reduced or no taxes to the federal government, even though they were unable—in fact, unwilling—to comply with the rule that they not discriminate in their admissions policies. In addition, donations made to the schools could be claimed as tax deductible by the people giving the money. Therefore, tuition payments were disguised as charitable donations by the white parents whose children attended those schools. This meant that they paid significantly lower income taxes than they would have without the so-called charitable contribution to the school.

Many African American parents whose children attended public schools in Memphis found out what the seg academies and their supporters were doing, and they were not happy. Almost thirty years after the Supreme Court ruled in *Brown v. Board of Education* that school segregation was unconstitutional, the Memphis public schools were deemed to be desegregating, or in the process of integrating, black and white students in these schools and, therefore, technically not breaking the law. However, the truth was that the desegregation of the public schools was meeting with great resistance and was therefore taking a long time to accomplish. Many black children attended schools that were virtually all black, while more and more white families were sending their children to private schools.

Inez Wright and her children had no interest in their attending a private school or academy. But they all understood the value of a successfully integrated public school system. Inez deeply believed that it was wrong for the federal government to encourage or support private schools that discriminated against students of color by giving them tax benefits and other types of government assistance (which could take the form of free textbooks, use of public spaces for school activities, etc.).

Inez contacted her local Legal Defense and Education Fund (LDEF), the legal branch of the NAACP (National Association for the Advancement of Colored People), and spoke with some of the lawyers there. They, in turn, discussed Inez's situation with colleagues in Washington, D.C.— lawyers at large private law firms who did volunteer *pro bono* work for groups like LDEF. Robert Kapp, one of those lawyers, agreed to take Inez's case along with several other cases, each of them focusing on discriminatory private schools in a different state. The lawyers understood that federal government support for segregated private schools in the form of tax benefits harmed the black families whose children attended the still-segregated public schools.

Inez Wright's case was *Wright v. Regan*. Donald Regan was, at that time, the Secretary of the U.S. Treasury and represented the Internal Revenue Service. The laws and policies of the IRS were being challenged. After losing in the U.S. district court, the federal trial court, Inez's lawyer appealed the decision to the next level, the U.S. Court of Appeals for the District of Columbia Circuit.

On June 18, 1981, a few days short of her first anniversary as a judge on that court, Ruth Bader Ginsburg delivered the court's opinion. She and the majority held that Inez and her children, and all the others in the same situation, had the right to ask a lower court to review the claim that they had been injured by the government's policies allowing discriminatory schools to enjoy tax benefits. Writing for the majority, Judge Ginsburg stated that Inez should have the opportunity to prove that the government's support of segregation, through the helpful tax laws used by the segregated private schools, "stigmatizes black schoolchildren and their parents by signaling official approbation of educational institutions that perpetuate in local communities notions, once prevalent in our nation, of the inferior quality of the black race." In other words, African American schoolchildren were being discriminated against because the tax rules seemed to be supportive of the segregated white schools by granting them special tax privileges.

Inez Wright and the other black parents were delighted by this ruling. But the decision was appealed by the IRS. This government agency argued that because the group of black parents were not directly affected by its tax-exemption policies, they did not have standing to sue. The black parents did not have children at the segregated schools and were therefore ineligible to bring a lawsuit against such practices. Three years later, the case reached the U.S. Supreme Court. In July 1984, the court overturned Judge Ginsburg's decision, agreeing with the "lack of standing" argument put forth by the IRS, so Inez Wright's lawsuit against the Internal Revenue Service had to be dropped. Inez was bitterly disappointed. She felt that her government was essentially saying, "It's OK to have segregated schools if you want to, and if you need help, we will help by funding segregated schools."

This was a painful defeat for all those who believed that it was wrong for the federal government to make it so attractive for white parents to send their children to segregated schools and to deprive African American children of the valuable experience of learning in integrated schools.

Many of the people involved in this fight had seen numerous examples of that kind of racial and ethnic segregation throughout their lives. Certainly Judge Ginsburg had.

Ruth Bader Ginsburg, lover of classical music and opera, never forgot the first time she sat in an audience surrounded by the beauty and drama of an opera performance. It was 1944, and she was eleven years old. Her aunt had taken her and a cousin to a special performance of a shortened version of the opera *La Gioconda* by Amilcare Ponchielli. The four acts of the original opera had been abridged to be performed in under one hour, so that the audience of children in the school auditorium could be attentive to the singing and the spoken explanations of the action onstage. The conductor and creator of this traveling mini-opera was a man named Dean Dixon.

Ruth learned from her aunt that Dean Dixon was doing something extraordinary. Justice Ginsburg explained many decades later that as an African American, "[Dixon] never was able to make a conducting career in the United States. He left for Europe, where he was very much appreciated." Dean Dixon, a highly accomplished conductor, had studied at the renowned Juilliard School and at Columbia University, both in New York City, where he also guest-conducted the NBC Symphony Orchestra and the New York Philharmonic. He was the first African American to lead these orchestras. However, "[as] an African-American, he was no more welcome in his native land as a conductor of major orchestras than African-Americans were accepted as players in Major League Baseball or on the stage of the Metropolitan Opera." In the 1940s, the United States was still an extraordinarily segregated country.

Ruth was sensitive to the racial discrimination she encountered at many points in her life. Even as a child, she understood that World War II, a dramatic international conflict that shaped her growing-up years, was not just a war the United States and its allies were fighting against the German Nazis and their allies, but also a war that at its core involved racism. She understood it as "a war in which people were exterminated on the basis of what other people called their race," referring to the extermination of Jews, Gypsies, and other groups by the Nazi regime.

Dean Dixon.

Ruth's commitment to equality was affirmed when she faced discrimination as a woman and as a Jew in her search for employment after graduating from law school. As a female law student, she had been part of a very visible minority. The handful of women in her law school class felt they were being held to different, even higher, standards than the male students. She would recall, "You felt that every eye was on you. Every time you answered a question, you felt you were answering for your entire sex. You were different and the object of curiosity." The same might be said about people of color when they are very much outnumbered by white people. In law schools of that period, the late 1950s, there were no women law professors or senior academic administrators. Not only were all professors male, but also they were all white. All deans, associate deans, and assistant deans were also white men.

Not surprisingly in this climate, not a single law firm offered Ruth Bader Ginsburg, a top-flight law school graduate, a position. "At Columbia, I was interviewed by a dozen firms. Only two asked me for follow-up interviews at their offices. And I didn't get an offer from either of them."

It is remarkable that she got as many interviews as she did, since at that time many employers explicitly stated they were interested only in male candidates. Ruth is often quoted as saying, "I had three strikes against me. First, I was Jewish, and the Wall Street firms were just beginning to accept Jews. Then I was a woman. But the killer was my daughter Jane, who was four by then." During that period, most law-firm employers were reluctant to hire a woman with children, fearing she would not stay at the job because of building a family or would neglect her duties because of responsibilities at home. At the same time, men with children were not viewed through the same lens.

Ruth Bader Ginsburg was conscious of being the object of discrimination because of her religion and her gender, and at the same time was aware of her own privilege as a white person. Years later, in discussing the lawsuits she brought through the ACLU in the 1970s, she acknowledged without hesitation the tremendous debt she owed the great Thurgood Marshall, a leader in the African American struggle for equality and the first African American appointed to the U.S. Supreme Court. It was under his guidance that *Brown v. Board of Education* (1954) was the first major success in the school desegregation effort. By the time that case reached the court, in the words of Ruth Bader Ginsburg, "It seemed inevitable that the Court would move in the direction it did. Marshall did not ask the Court to take a giant stride. A step-by-step was his successful strategy." She stated proudly that her own successful legal strategy over the years had been modeled on his. At the same time, Justice Ginsburg rejected any comparison between herself and Justice Marshall: "His life was on the line when he went to a small town in the South. My life was never in danger." In her law school classes, as in her judicial opinions later, Ruth Bader Ginsburg taught "how wrong it is to judge people on the basis of the color of their skin."

When Ruth Bader Ginsburg became active with the ACLU, she did so out of a desire to put into practice some of the basic legal principles she had learned as a student and taught as a law professor. She wanted to commit herself to working to protect people's civil liberties and civil rights.

This commitment was very meaningful during Professor Ginsburg's early law school teaching years. The 1960s and 1970s were characterized by a growing wave of actions by thousands and thousands of people, young and old, women and men, of all races and ethnicities and faiths, who were demanding an end to racial segregation, in the South and throughout the country. There were demonstrations for racial equality in cities large and small across the United States; there were lawsuits in the courts at local, state, and national levels; and there were major organizing campaigns to support African Americans in the areas most affected by the so-called Jim Crow laws, local and state laws that mandated separate schools, drinking fountains, movie theater seats, restaurants, libraries, restrooms, swimming pools, hotels, and entrances to and exits from buildings for African Americans and white Americans.

Like all progressive people, especially lawyers, Ruth Bader Ginsburg knew that a crucial area of discrimination addressed during the early 1960s was that of voting rights throughout the South. Many southern states enacted "grandfather clauses," laws aimed at keeping former slaves and their descendants from voting. Some states created voter eligibility "tests" that would have been impossible for anyone to pass, such as estimating correctly the number of jelly beans in a jar (without taking them out to hand-count them) or the number of bubbles that a bar of soap would produce. In some places, illegal fees were charged before people could exercise the right to vote.

Among the best-known acts of protest against the widespread disenfranchisement of so many citizens were the three marches from Selma,

Alabama, to Montgomery, Alabama, in March 1965. The first march, on March 7, started peacefully. One of the heroes of that day was young John Lewis. He led the march and recalls, "There were no big names up front, no celebrities. This was just plain folks moving through the streets of Selma."

Like people throughout the United States, Ruth Bader Ginsburg was deeply aware of the events that occurred at that historic march once the participants reached the Edmund Pettus Bridge, which spans the Alabama River. As they peacefully crossed the bridge, they were attacked by blue-uniformed Alabama state troopers with billy clubs, and other armed men. John Lewis was very badly beaten, as were dozens of others.

John Lewis in 1964.

Two other marches followed, led by the Reverend Martin Luther King, Jr. By mid-March of 1965, there was national outrage at the rampant use of violence against people who were merely exercising their constitutional rights to speak, protest, and assemble. Around the country, multiple acts of civil disobedience occurred, as well as demonstrations in all major cities. President Lyndon B. Johnson urgently asked that his proposed Voting Rights Act be passed by Congress immediately.

On August 6, 1965, President Johnson signed the Voting Rights Act into law. The new law made it illegal for any state to place obstacles in the way of eligible voters exercising their right to be politically active, to register to vote, and to vote for the candidate of their choice. There could be no discrimination in voting based on a person's race. Most important, the act required states with a history of discrimination against African American and other minority voters to obtain written approval from the federal government whenever they wanted to make changes in their state and local election laws. This act was extended by four subsequent presidents.

Between the first time Ruth Bader Ginsburg took on a case to protect a person's civil rights (around 1969 or 1970) and her appointment to the Supreme Court (1993), the rights of African American citizens to vote were under constant attack. Many changes in voter ID laws mandated certain types of ID that were difficult if not impossible for many citizens to acquire. When these regulations have been legally challenged, courts have determined that they are designed specifically to prevent African American and minority citizens from exercising their right to vote.

These developments affecting citizens' voting rights were of central interest to lawyers and legal scholars like Ruth Bader Ginsburg. Even before she became a judge and then a justice, she was exposed to a wide variety of litigation challenging the restrictive laws aimed at reducing the number of African American and minority voters. In the early 1960s, Professor

Ginsburg began working on more and more cases for the ACLU. The organization provided legal representation directly to people involved in the struggle for voting rights in the South and for an end to racial discrimination everywhere in the United States. The ACLU represented African American students who sat in at a segregated department store in North Carolina, other students arrested for demonstrating in various southern states, and courageous African American students who integrated schools and universities. In 1964, the ACLU opened an office in Atlanta, Georgia, to focus on southern civil rights matters.

Almost fifty years later, Justice Ruth Bader Ginsburg would write the outraged dissent in *Shelby County, Alabama v. Holder* (2013). This case came to the Supreme Court because the authorities of Shelby County, Alabama, challenged the right of the U.S. Congress to extend the Voting Rights Act for an additional twenty-five years. Congress was going to extend the act because extensive studies had found continued violations of people's right to vote throughout the country. Shelby County was resisting the idea that certain states would still need the federal government's approval (called *preclearance*) before changing their voting laws.

By a majority vote of five to four, the U.S. Supreme Court ruled that the federal approval section of the Voting Rights Act would no longer apply, giving all the states the right to make any changes they wanted in their voting laws without obtaining preclearance from the federal government.

Justice Ginsburg vigorously and heatedly disagreed with this outcome, as did three of her colleagues, Justices Stephen G. Breyer, Sonia Sotomayor, and Elena Kagan. The four dissenters asserted that there was much too much evidence that the southern states with the worst past records of voting-rights violations were still acting to reduce the number of African American and minority voters. Therefore, the act needed to retain the preclearance—prior approval—requirement.

Justice Ginsburg was so incensed by the majority opinion that she did something quite rare in the Supreme Court: she read a summary of her dissenting opinion out loud from the bench. Her wrath can be felt through the carefully selected words of her dissent: "The sad irony of today's decision lies in its utter failure to grasp why the Voting Rights Act has proven effective. Throwing out preclearance when it has worked and is continuing to work to stop discriminatory changes is like throwing away your umbrella in a rainstorm because you are not getting wet. The Court's opinion can hardly be described as an exemplar of restrained and moderate decision making. Quite the opposite. Hubris [arrogance that can lead to a downfall] is a fit word for today's demolition of the Voting Rights Act. In my judgment, the Court errs egregiously."

Echoing Justice Ginsburg's dissent, Congressman John Lewis declared, "The Supreme Court has stuck a dagger into the heart of the Voting Rights Act. These men never stood in unmovable lines. They were never denied the right to participate in the democratic process. They were never beaten, jailed, run off their farms or fired from their jobs. No one they knew died simply trying to register to vote."

These two people, Justice Ruth Bader Ginsburg and Congressman John Lewis, had grown to maturity in very different circumstances but in the same country, and they had responded in parallel ways to the injustices they each experienced and witnessed. Both early on developed passionate convictions about the need to fight for equality between women and men, between people of color and white people, believing that the words "with liberty and justice for all" in the Pledge of Allegiance, which reflect the promises of the Declaration of Independence, should be a lived reality for every person in this country.

Opposition to discrimination in all its forms is present in the bulk of Ruth Bader Ginsburg's professional work. As a judge on the U.S. Court of

Appeals for the D.C. Circuit, she strongly supported Inez Wright and her children, ruling that they had shown they were harmed by the IRS's giving privileges to segregated private schools. Years later, Supreme Court Justice Ginsburg continued to stand in favor of the rights of African Americans to live as equal citizens without being discriminated against as voters. She worked hard to support other constitutionally protected freedoms as well. She became known for her progressive positions on matters of free speech, free association, and freedom from discrimination of every kind.

NINE

WOMEN'S RIGHTS ARE HUMAN RIGHTS

I N EARLY 1970, a young woman living in Perth Amboy, New Jersey, took a step that would turn out to be tremendously significant for her personally as well as for hundreds if not thousands of other women in situations like hers. Her name was Nora Simon, and she was twenty-four years old.

Nora Simon was born in 1946 to a French mother and an American father who at the time was in the United States Army stationed in France. At some point, Nora and her parents moved back to the United States and lived with or near her paternal grandparents. They were a working-class family, and Nora grew up with modest ambitions. One of her strongest desires was to serve her country in the military, just as her father had.

In early 1967, at the age of twenty-one, Nora had enlisted in the army, specifically in the Women's Army Corps. Because she had trained as a practical nurse in preparation for her military service, Nora was able to enlist as a medical specialist. She was assigned to serve at Fort Ord, California, where she successfully completed basic training. She was recognized as a dedicated and diligent worker and soon earned the praise of her superiors. She did so well, in fact, that she was chosen to be a barrack sergeant, a position that placed her in charge of a military living quarters.

And then life happened to Nora. She fell in love with an army officer who had the unusual name of Ulyess Douglas Price. Nora was twenty-two; Ulyess was twenty. Shortly after their marriage in June 1968, they discovered that Nora was pregnant. Because of army regulations at the time, she immediately received an honorable discharge. She would never be eligible for reenlistment in the Women's Army Corps. She could not even request a waiver of the rule. Although he was soon to be a father, Ulyess was permitted to remain an officer in the army.

The young couple moved to Sollie Trailer Park in Ozark, Alabama, near the base where Ulyess was performing his military service. In January 1969, Nora gave birth to a baby boy, who was named after his father. A few months later, the marriage between Nora and Ulyess was legally annulled and the baby boy was given up for adoption. Since she was now both single and childless, Nora believed she would once again be eligible to enlist in the Women's Army Corps.

But Nora discovered that the army regulation barring her from reenlisting would be very difficult to overcome. She learned this when, shortly after returning to Perth Amboy, New Jersey, without either a husband or a child, she attempted to reenlist in the United States Army and was denied. The prohibition against reenlisting could be removed only in cases where a pregnancy ended in a miscarriage or a newborn child died shortly after birth. Neither situation was true for Nora.

Not to be deterred, Nora next tried to enlist in the United States Navy. Though she successfully passed all the written and physical tests, Nora's application was denied by the navy, too. She contacted her congressional representative, without results.

Nora Simon was nothing if not persistent. Somewhere along the way, she had familiarized herself with the few antidiscrimination laws existing at that time, in particular the Civil Rights Act of 1964. Title VII of that law specifically forbids discrimination based on gender in hiring, so long as both a female and a male candidate for a job have the same required qualifications. Nora was convinced that the Women's Army Corps was violating her rights under the Civil Rights Act, and she wanted to do something about it.

Nora contacted the ACLU, first in a letter to the main office in Washington, D.C., and then in communications to the New Jersey affiliate. She stated her position clearly: "I am supposed to get equal rights for a job for which I am qualified!" Although her letters were initially filed away for future reference, her letter of April 13, 1970, was forwarded to the Rutgers law professor Ruth Bader Ginsburg. It was just the type of case the ACLU volunteer attorney liked to take on, and she agreed to help Nora Simon.

Although the case seemed quite straightforward, winning it was by no means guaranteed. Nora had stated, "I am fully ready to go to court." But Ruth Bader Ginsburg hoped the army would agree to change its policy for all women in situations like Nora's, keeping the case out of the courts. Approaching the situation strategically, she wrote to the army, waited patiently for a response to her letter, and finally put the letter into a format that could become a formal complaint should she and Nora decide to commence a lawsuit. In addition to her initial letter, she contacted many other people about the glaring example of gender discrimination in the armed services exposed by Nora's situation. She wrote to politicians and lawyers, to judges and professors. Professor Ginsburg did draft a formal complaint but never delivered it to representatives of the army.

By October 1970, her strategy began to pay off. Responding to pressure, the army informed her that Nora Simon would be allowed to reenlist under a special dispensation, while they continued to work on plans to change the regulation once and for all. Eventually the military abolished the regulation.

Sally Reed as a young woman.

At the center of another of Ruth Bader Ginsburg's earliest cases was another modest, unassuming woman. Her name was Sally Reed. Like so many of Professor Ginsburg's clients, Sally Reed was an ordinary person who did something extraordinary: she challenged a law that she felt was unfair.

Sally Reed's story was happening in Idaho just around the time that Charles Moritz's case (chapter six) was unfolding in Colorado and Nora Simon's (earlier this chapter) was developing in New Jersey. In 1970, Charles Moritz had challenged the law that did not recognize his role as caregiver to his aged mother and entitle him to a tax benefit. As the mother of a nineteen-year-old son who died tragically, Sally Reed was not ready to accept that she was automatically disqualified as the administrator of the boy's tiny estate ($485 and a few personal effects), while the boy's father was automatically appointed. Charles and Sally were both lucky to be represented by Ruth Bader Ginsburg.

And while the *Moritz* case ended in victory in the federal appeals court in Colorado, Sally Reed's case (*Reed v. Reed*) went all the way to the Supreme Court in 1971. It was decided unanimously in favor of Sally Reed. The court found that a law automatically giving "preference to members of either sex over members of the other is forbidden by the Equal Protection Clause of the Fourteenth Amendment."

This clause requires that all people in the United States receive equal and fair treatment by official bodies such as governments, schools, military forces, and local and state agencies. Any distinctions between different groups of people have to be reasonable and not based specifically on race, ethnicity, religion, or gender, unless there is some clear reason for the different treatment.

The year 1970 also brought Ruth Bader Ginsburg a case that would be seen as crucial to the development of her strategic vision of fighting for gender equality. The case involved a young woman named Sharron Perry.

Sharron was born into a large, close-knit family in Greenfield, Massachusetts. Her grandmother was an important influence in her life. Sharron recalled her as "the most powerful person" and "the best educated and [most] career-oriented person" in her family. Seeing the older woman succeed and thrive as a rehabilitation nurse, Sharron decided she wanted to follow in her footsteps.

Sharron wanted to go to a four-year college, but like many working-class and blue-collar families, her family could not afford the cost of tuition for all four years. So, in her senior year of college, Sharron joined the military. She applied for and received a special scholarship to pay for her final year in college. She was commissioned as a second lieutenant in the United States Air Force and was awarded a bachelor of science degree in physical therapy at the University of Connecticut. Sharron was proud to be the second person in her extended family to earn a college degree.

Sharron graduated from college in October 1969 and was immediately posted to Maxwell Air Force Base in Montgomery, Alabama, where she would work as a physical

Sharron Perry's high school picture.

therapist in the base hospital. On December 27, 1969, Sharron and her fiancé, Joseph Frontiero, married. Joseph, a military veteran, was going to school full-time at Huntingdon College in Montgomery. Because he had completed his military service, Joseph received financial assistance from the GI Bill, the law that provides benefits to military veterans. With this help, Joseph was able to attend school when he returned to civilian life. Sharron was aware that the air force gave married service members extra pay to help cover housing costs and also provided medical and dental benefits for their spouses. So, early in 1970, after she had informed the air force of her recent marriage, Sharron was distressed to see that the additional housing allowance was not reflected in her paycheck. Certain that this was a clerical error, she went directly to the payroll office.

Sharron received a shock. There had been no clerical error. The military had a specific policy that permitted them to treat male and female service members differently. Married men in the service automatically received an extra housing allowance and health benefits for their wives, even if the wife worked or had independent income of her own. But married women in the service received no such automatic benefits. The female service member had to prove that her husband was dependent on her, which meant proving that he relied on her for more than half of his financial support. For the young Frontiero couple, the math just didn't work out; Joe's monthly income was almost fifty dollars a month over the allowable amount for the spouse of a female service member. They did not qualify for the additional benefit.

Sharron knew that her married male colleagues, doing the same work as she was, were receiving the benefit, and she thought the distinction was unfair. Others saw it differently. She reported, "I had people telling me, 'You're lucky we let you into the military at all.' And then I got mad!" She found Joseph Levin, a lawyer at the Southern Poverty Law Center in

Sharron (Perry) Frontiero in the U.S. Air Force.

Montgomery, who agreed to take her case. They filed a lawsuit against the government on December 23, 1970, four days before the Frontieros' first wedding anniversary.

At the time of Sharron's initial lawsuit, the armed forces had two hundred thousand male officers and one million enlisted men. There were only six thousand married women in the service, so their issues with discriminatory policies were easy for the military establishment to dismiss.

However, among these women were a small but growing number who had managed to reach the higher ranks in the military. One of these was Major General Jeanne M. Holm, an air force officer who for many years had been struggling to change the rules, policies, and practices that

Major General Jeanne M. Holm, the first woman to serve at that grade in the U.S. Armed Forces.

negatively affected women in the service. Based on her experiences, she knew that the only way change would happen was through the courts. And she let it be known that if there were a lawsuit, she would help as much as she could with all the information and insight she had in her power. Major General Holm had in fact been communicating with Professor Ginsburg a few years earlier about the Nora Simon case and others like it.

On January 17, 1973, a little more than two years after Sharron Frontiero started her legal action against the government's discriminatory policies, Ruth Bader Ginsburg joined Sharron's Southern Poverty Law Center lawyer Joseph Levin to argue the case for her position in front of the justices of the U.S. Supreme Court.

It was a big day. For Sharron Frontiero, it was the culmination of her efforts to bring some sort of equality to the policies of the United States Armed Forces. For all the women facing similar situations, it was a moment that might prove to be critical to their futures, depending on how the Supreme Court eventually decided. And for Ruth Bader Ginsburg, who had only once before stood up in a courtroom to argue an appeal—in the U.S. Court of Appeals for the Tenth Circuit, in the *Moritz* case—it was momentous because it was her first Supreme Court oral argument. She never forgot that day. "I was terribly nervous. In fact, I didn't eat lunch for fear that I might throw up." However, her meticulous preparation and her confidence in the soundness of her arguments prevailed. "Two minutes into my argument, the fear dissolved. Suddenly, I realized that here before me were the nine leading jurists of America, a captive audience. I felt a surge of power that carried me through."

Ruth Bader Ginsburg's confidence was well placed. As she presented her carefully constructed argument, none of the nine Supreme Court justices interrupted her with a question. Not a single one! In her argument, this future Supreme Court justice explained carefully that gender was similar to race. She referenced the Equal Protection Clause of the Fourteenth Amendment to the U.S. Constitution, which protects people from being treated differently because of gender or race. She enumerated the various ways women at that time faced discrimination at all levels of society, even though statistically women outnumbered men in the country's population. In other words, she explained, you don't have to be a member of a minority group in order to suffer unconstitutional discrimination. She concluded by saying she was not suggesting that women be treated *better* than men. She quoted the noted nineteenth-century abolitionist and women's rights activist Sarah Grimké, who said: "I ask no favor for my sex. All I ask of our brethren is that they take their feet off our necks."

Ruth Bader Ginsburg's contributions to the Supreme Court appeal, including her *amicus* brief and her sharp and well-organized oral argument, convinced eight of the nine Supreme Court justices to vote in favor of Sharron Frontiero. On May 14, 1973, the court held that the laws and regulations the air force had used to deny Sharron Frontiero the same benefits as her married male colleagues were a violation of the Constitution.

As the struggle for women's rights grew into a mass movement starting in the early 1970s, the courtroom was a central arena. Across the United States, women individually and in groups were finding their voices and demanding to be heard, frequently through lawsuits challenging discriminatory laws. Lawyers, mostly women and some men, began offering their services and expertise to women who challenged being treated as second-class citizens in the pay they received, the promotions they got or should have gotten, the jobs open or closed to them, and the support provided them by different governmental structures and laws. Professionals were looking closely at all the laws on the books at every level of government, as well as membership requirements in schools and universities, clubs, and other organizations.

In 1972, Professor Ginsburg had helped to launch the Women's Rights Project at the ACLU. This group aimed to identify and take on legal challenges to the widespread gender distinctions embedded in the law, hoping to centralize, to some extent, the kind of legal work that was already proliferating in all parts of the nation. Ruth Bader Ginsburg's approach was intended to persuade the justices on the U.S. Supreme Court that laws distinguishing between men and women simply on gender grounds were bad for both women and men. She used a carefully thought through line of attack, selecting cases she felt confident of winning, even if each one on its own might seem not particularly significant to some. She took trouble to sequence the types of cases she took on.

In all the cases she brought, Ruth Bader Ginsburg litigated, step by step, against the laws that relied on unreasonable or irrational distinctions between men and women. Even distinctions that didn't seem at first glance to be important assumed more significance when placed in the broader context. So it was, for example, in what was widely and jokingly called the Beer Case (*Craig v. Boren,* 1976). At the time of the lawsuit, Curtis Craig was a student at Oklahoma State University and David Boren was the governor of Oklahoma. The issue was an Oklahoma law stating that all women age eighteen and over were allowed to buy a particular kind of low-alcohol beer, while men had to be twenty-one years old to buy it.

The case originated with an underage college freshman and a young woman friend of his who wanted to buy some beer to take to a party. Because he was under twenty-one, he had to step aside while his date, also under twenty-one but over eighteen, bought the beer. They thought this was unfair and unreasonable. Yes, this case was "just about buying beer," but it was based on the important principle that no kind of gender or race discrimination should exist, in either direction.

By the time the case reached the U.S. Supreme Court, Ruth Bader Ginsburg had joined the legal team representing the young people and had written an *amicus curiae* brief

Professor Ginsburg as a scholar in residence at the Rockefeller Foundation in Bellagio, Italy, 1977.

that was intended to persuade the justices that the Oklahoma law was discriminatory and therefore unlawful.

And it worked! Seven of the nine Supreme Court justices found that gender classifications such as that reflected in the Oklahoma beer law were unconstitutional and violated the Equal Protection Clause of the Fourteenth Amendment. For the first time, the court used a test called *heightened scrutiny* in examining the law as it affected women and men, requiring the Oklahoma state government to show that different treatment of men and women under a particular law was serving an important state goal and was reasonably related to that goal. In the Beer Case, differentiating between eighteen-year-old women and twenty-one-year-old men for purposes of buying low-alcohol beer was called "invidious

Professor Ginsburg at the time of her nomination to the federal bench.

discrimination" against males eighteen to twenty years old, serving no important purpose for the state of Oklahoma. As such, it was unconstitutional. The groundwork for all similar cases in the late 1970s was being laid in the early part of the decade in the work Ruth Bader Ginsburg was doing on such cases as Nora Simon's and Sharron Frontiero's.

Less than four years after the Beer Case, on June 30, 1980, Ruth Bader Ginsburg was sworn in as a judge on the U.S. Court of Appeals for the District of Columbia Circuit—a federal judge. She had been appointed by President Jimmy Carter. President Carter had made it very clear that he wasn't happy that the judges in most United States courts "all look like me," male and white. He went about appointing women and people of color to many vacant positions on the various federal courts in the United States. When Jimmy Carter took office in 1977, only six of the 497 federal judges were women. By the time he left office in 1981, he had appointed forty more women as federal judges. And one of those forty was Ruth Bader Ginsburg.

When Judge and later Justice Ginsburg received groups of school-children in her courtroom, she was invariably asked whether she had always wanted to be a judge. The question made her laugh, "because in the days that I went to law school, only one woman in the history of the United States had ever been a federal appeals court judge." And, of course, until 1981, when Sandra Day O'Connor was appointed a justice of the U.S. Supreme Court, there had never been a woman on that highest court in the land. So, explained Ruth Bader Ginsburg, it was not until she heard President Jimmy Carter speak about wanting to make the federal bench look more like the country it served that she even contemplated the possibility of becoming a judge.

President Carter's vision of a more diverse and broadly representative bench reflected the climate of the period. The women's movement was in full swing by 1980, and long-held views and attitudes and opinions about gender were being challenged and changed both in and out of court. All through the 1970s, a movement was in process to find new ways of using old laws and policies to bring about greater equality for all. And very often, because an old law or policy could not be adequately altered, it had to be thrown out and a new one enacted.

During the years leading up to her appointment to the court of appeals, Professor Ruth Ginsburg further developed her strategy for reforming legislation that governed how women and men were treated in society, its

The four women who had risen to the Supreme Court—from left, Justices Sandra Day O'Connor, Sonia Sotomayor, Ruth Bader Ginsburg, and Elena Kagan —photographed at Justice Kagan's investiture.

institutions, and its laws. At Rutgers Law School, Professor Ginsburg handled many ACLU-supported cases with outcomes that had far-reaching effects. Some of her cases challenged existing laws and practices: the requirement on certain official forms to indicate gender where that information was irrelevant to the purpose of the form; discrimination in tax deductions; discriminatory policies regarding the uniforms that employees of the U.S. Postal Service were required to wear; the right of married women to retain or regain their birth surnames; the discriminatory nature of "Ladies' Day at the Movies," where women were charged less than men for a movie ticket on a certain day of the week; sexist language in the questions on certain state bar examinations.

In one significant series of cases, Professor Ginsburg challenged university-run enrichment programs that admitted high school boys but not girls. Princeton University's Upward Bound Summer Program had been established to provide educational advantages to boys living in poor local areas, but not girls. Another, similar program also run by Princeton University offered exposure to engineering for underprivileged sixth- through eighth-grade boys, but not for girls. The directors of both programs experienced Professor Ginsburg's persistent pressure, through letters, meetings, and public statements. Her message was simple: separate was not equal. Girls needed to have the identical opportunities boys had, in exactly the same setting, with exactly the same offerings. Ultimately, the programs stopped discriminating against girls.

When Professor Ginsburg moved to Columbia Law School in 1972, she continued her involvement in local matters that presented situations of gender discrimination. One such case arose in 1972, when the university announced it would be dismissing twenty of the women, mostly black and Latina, who worked as maids, cleaning the buildings, bathrooms, and offices on the New York City campus. At the same time, the university was hiring male janitors to do the same jobs, though the administration claimed that the skills required for a janitor's job were different from those required for a maid's job. Working with the ACLU and other supporters on campus, Professor Ginsburg and the union representing the maids were successful in halting the firing. The women kept their jobs and received a wage increase.

With the Women's Rights Project of the ACLU, Ruth Bader Ginsburg was active in more than two dozen lawsuits that went to court, as well as countless others where a non-litigated outcome—a settlement—was possible. These cases involved issues such as discrimination in employment, pregnancy, jury service, unemployment benefits, alimony, and college

admissions. The rights of both men and women were protected and/or expanded by these cases, even where there was not an actual courtroom victory. Simply airing the ideas and positions exposed in a wide variety of situations was a tremendous contribution to the ongoing social discussion of gender equality.

In 1993, Judge Ruth Bader Ginsburg of the U.S. Court of Appeals for the D.C. Circuit was nominated to a seat on the Supreme Court of the United States. She was confirmed by the United States Senate (ninety-six to three) in August of that year, becoming the second woman ever to sit on the highest court in the land. She joined Justice Sandra Day O'Connor, who had been the lone woman on that court since her appointment by President Ronald Reagan in 1981. Could the high school, college, and law student Ruth Bader Ginsburg ever have imagined that she would occupy such a position?

By the time of her confirmation hearings in 1993, she was energized, excited, and ready to meet the challenge. It was "an opportunity beyond any other for one of my training to serve society," she declared in her formal testimony before the Senate. She viewed it as "the highest honor, the most awesome trust, that can be placed in a judge."

When Justice Ginsburg was in her third term—third year—on the Supreme Court, in 1996, she had the opportunity to write an opinion for the majority that was the culmination of her long-term effort to win equal protection and treatment for women and men. It was also the signal that a new era of greater acceptance of equality was beginning.

The case (*United States v. Virginia*) had taken several years to reach the Supreme Court. The Virginia Military Institute, a public institution, did not admit women. In 1989, a young woman high school student had

Judge Ginsburg during her first term.

applied to the VMI, and her application had not even been opened, let alone reviewed and then rejected. She complained about this to the United States Department of Justice (DOJ), which agreed to investigate the matter. Ultimately, the DOJ sued the state of Virginia, maintaining that the overt gender discrimination in the school's policies was unconstitutional and not permissible under the law.

Because VMI had a long, glorious history in Virginia, the courts there were not friendly to the U.S. government's position. The case traveled to several different levels of the federal court system before landing with the Supreme Court for a final decision. The spokesmen for the military academy made a good effort to justify the single-sex admission policy. However, the Supreme Court justices in their majority (seven of them, with one justice recusing himself and another dissenting) looked closely at the question of whether Virginia "can constitutionally deny to women who have the will and capacity, the training and attendant opportunities that VMI uniquely affords." They concluded that the answer had to be no, that any woman who had "the will and capacity" should have the opportunity to apply and be considered for admission to VMI. The VMI decision was revolutionary, bringing to the forefront the constitutional right to equality in education for women and men, a position Justice Ginsburg had strongly upheld when as an ACLU volunteer lawyer she had fought for educational equality for children in university enrichment programs so many decades earlier.

Although the chief justice had assigned Ruth's colleague Justice O'Connor to write the majority opinion, Justice O'Connor recognized that the relevant area of the law was near and dear to her sister jurist's heart. She was also aware that Justice Ginsburg was the appropriate author for the opinion because of her many years of experience litigating

Judge Ginsburg is sworn in as Justice Ginsburg. Chief Justice William H. Rehnquist (left) administered the oath; Judge Ginsburg's husband, Marty Ginsburg, held the Bible sworn on during the ceremony.

equal-protection cases. "This should be Ruth's," said Justice O'Connor as she gave the assignment to her colleague. It would become one of Justice Ginsburg's most significant opinions.

Nora Simon must have felt proud when she learned of that decision. Twenty-three years earlier, in December 1973, Ruth Bader Ginsburg had written Nora a letter that included these words: "I have thought of you many times during these years of controversy over differential treatment of men and women in the armed services. When the battle is won (we're coming closer every day), ACLU will write up the full story and you will be featured as one of the brave women who emerged when most were afraid to complain." Nora's complaint had been heard by someone who could and did do something about it. All through the United States, women and men enjoy greater freedom and equality because of individuals like Nora Simon, Sharron Frontiero, and the many unnamed women and girls who spoke up about being shut out of schools or programs of study because of their gender.

TEN

Blazing a Trail, Leaving Her Mark

S YDNEY KEGAN BRANNOCH was a curious child. She was born on March 27, 1987, and when she was quite young, she started pestering her family and teachers with questions: How do things work? Why do they do what they do? Where can we find out about them? Who determines the answers to these kinds of questions?

Sydney's family supported her in her search for answers by giving her many enrichment opportunities. She was a voracious reader, especially fond of *National Geographic* magazine and her family's collection of encyclopedias. The family took camping trips and traveled to many parts of the United States outside of the northeastern region where she grew up. Sydney said later, "Early childhood exposure to the natural world blossomed into a teenage inquisitiveness that pulled me in many directions." In high school, Sydney continued to devour "book after book," and as her curiosity grew, she began to wonder about how much each person's view and understanding of the world depended on whether the person was female or male, rich or poor, of color or white.

While studying philosophy in college, Sydney "took an entomology class on a whim because I wanted to learn more about insects. This class

Sydney Brannoch in her lab.

opened my eyes to the overwhelming diversity of insects." In 2014 Sydney enrolled in a PhD program at Case Western Reserve University in Cleveland, Ohio, where she was able to follow her passion, pursuing entomology.

While Sydney and her peers were growing up and preparing for college, there were significantly fewer young women than men going into the sciences. Even where there were slow improvements, it was still true that at the higher levels of instruction and leadership, most scientific fields were dominated by men. Just as Ruth Bader Ginsburg had struggled to find role models as she entered a field that was atypical for women and unwelcoming to them, Sydney and students like her looked for guidance to support them in their decision to enter areas of study and professions that were not historically considered "women's work."

Many young women who were entering fields that had been closed to women, including the aspiring entomologist Sydney, were encouraged by following the careers of path makers like Justice Ginsburg. They admired women like her and those whom she represented, and they emulated her persistence and strength, just as when she was a girl Justice Ginsburg had admired Amelia Earhart, the pioneering aviator, for her courage, daring, and sense of adventure. Sydney began learning about Ruth Bader Ginsburg's life. She said, "Without Ruth Bader Ginsburg, I don't know if many women would be able to pursue their dreams as easily or as freely."

As Sydney, a questioner by nature, advanced in her studies of the insect world, where male specimens were consistently used to classify all insect species, she eventually asked herself "why female specimens weren't used to define most species." So, to test a theory she sensed was correct, Sydney and her thesis adviser, Dr. Gavin Svenson, examined thirty praying mantis specimens. They were able to show definitively that these mantises could be classified by species on the basis of their female characteristics, not just the male mantises' characteristics. In the course of their study, Sydney and Dr. Svenson identified a new species of mantis. Sydney named her newly discovered insect *Ilomantis ginsburgae* in honor of Justice Ruth Bader Ginsburg.

Sydney Brannoch was one of many people who showed their admiration for Justice Ginsburg in unexpected and creative ways. To her own surprise, Justice Ruth Bader

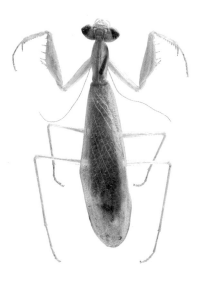

Ilomantis ginsburgae, the insect named in honor of Justice Ginsburg.

Ginsburg became a popular media and cultural icon for a widely diverse audience. Much of her visibility and popularity grew out of a Tumblr blog created in the spring of 2013 by a law student named Shana Knizhnik. Shana called her blog *Notorious R.B.G.* because she wanted to honor Ruth Bader Ginsburg for her principled and searing dissent in the voting-rights case *Shelby County v. Holder,* as well as for other dissents for which she had become known. Moved by her own deep outrage at the majority decision in *Shelby,* which effectively eliminated many protections of the right of citizens to vote freely, Shana remembered reading Justice Ginsburg's advice about not giving in to feelings of anger, since those feelings "sap energy better devoted to productive endeavors." Shana got creative with her blog, which also paid tribute to the memory of the rapper and hip-hop artist Notorious B.I.G. *Notorious R.B.G.* became an overnight sensation and eventually a book.

The blog introduced RBG T-shirts, which sold out very fast. Soon other people picked up on the idea, and RBG merchandise galore followed: not just various T-shirts with a wide variety of pictures of the justice, but also mugs, temporary tattoos, children's RBG dress-up costumes, an adult Halloween costume as "Ruth Vader Ginsburg" (including the *Star Wars* Darth Vader helmet and the Ginsburg black gown and lacy jabot or collar), kitchen aprons, greeting cards, onesies and bibs for babies, tank-tops, and coloring books.

Along with the merchandise, dozens if not hundreds of filmed, recorded, and printed interviews with Justice Ginsburg, articles and books about her, and articles by her, as well as an autobiographical book, *My Own Words,* appeared in print. These interviews and writings opened a window on her life and her principles to people across the nation and abroad. Her level of celebrity, a first for a U.S. Supreme Court justice, demonstrates that her contributions to profound and lasting social change, especially in the area of gender equality, found a vast army of supporters and admirers. The fact that her elevation to virtual star status happened when she was in her eighties is a good sign that ageism is not universal.

In addition to her widespread base of fans and admirers, Justice Ruth Bader Ginsburg's law clerks were among her most loyal and devoted supporters. The experience of spending a year essentially as her apprentice but also as her colleague was transformative and, for many, inspirational.

The RBG bobblehead figure featured in *The Green Bag, An Entertaining Journal of Law.*

Justice Ginsburg's former clerks pointed to her work ethic as a powerful influence in their own professional lives. One of them recalled that the justice would work until well past midnight on the cases they were preparing. Another remarked with admiration on her phenomenal memory for the details of dozens of cases at a time. And yet another characterized the justice as a perfectionist when it came to her own work.

Another common theme among her former law clerks was what they learned from her about professionalism. They agreed that the justice's focus on good, clear, succinct writing helped them tremendously to advance in their careers. "She trained me well, and taught me that language matters," said her former law clerk Neil Siegel, who went on to become a law professor. Margo Schlanger, who also became a law professor after her clerkship, called the justice "an amazing presence. She is so smart, and so dedicated, and so hard-working that it sets an example for you to live up to for the rest of your career."

The law clerks learned from Justice Ginsburg's example that "it's always about the case, not about egos," said Neil Siegel. With the justice, recalled Linda Lye, who went on to work with the ACLU in California, they honed their analytical skills, learning that "command of the big picture must be coupled with mastery of detail." All of the justice's law clerks emulated her emphasis on hard work and precision in their later professional endeavors.

Finally, all of Justice Ginsburg's law clerks were touched by her warmth, her generosity, her compassion, and the way her life comported with her deeply held belief in equality and fairness. The law clerks who knew her husband, Marty, recalled how moving it was to witness their truly egalitarian marriage. That relationship of equals served as inspiration for their own marriages. Former law clerks experienced the justice's commitment to collegiality in the atmosphere in chambers. Linda Lye commented that Justice Ginsburg hired clerks who are not only "smart, diligent, and do a good job," but are also "good and decent human beings."

While to the general public Justice Ginsburg may have seemed stern, unsmiling, perhaps even dour, those close to her saw her differently. One of her clerks described her big personality, while another highlighted her great sense of humor. Although the time that these law clerks spent in Justice Ginsburg's chambers was primarily devoted to work, there was ample space for family needs, for joyful gatherings, for kindness and good humor.

Justice Ginsburg showed her fondness for her extended family of law clerks in various ways. When one of them, or any other staff member in chambers, had a birthday, there was invariably some sort of party. Up until his death, the justice's chef supreme, Marty, baked the celebratory cake. Traveling always meant returning with gifts for her clerks. When former clerks married, the justice sent them gifts, and their children also received tokens of her affection on their birthdays. Her former law clerk Neil Siegel described Justice Ginsburg's consistent interest in his children as "generous and supportive in ways that matter. It has meant a great deal to me that she is a part of my daughters' lives."

The justice took her clerks on field trips to the opera or concerts, invited them to her home for elegant dinners, and was always responsive to their personal needs. Just as she maintained contact with former clients like Stephen Wiesenfeld and Sharron (Frontiero) Cohen, Justice Ginsburg stayed in touch with her law clerks after they moved on, remaining interested in their professional growth and helpful to them when needed. She mentored them with enthusiasm and affection.

Justice Ginsburg with Sharron (Frontiero) Cohen, left, and Jason Wiesenfeld, 2004.

Several of Justice Ginsburg's former law clerks described her as being tough, both in her approach to her work and in dealing with a life that was not always easy. Of very spare build that appeared frail with age, Justice Ginsburg's toughness extended to taking care of her body and her health. From the age of twenty-nine, she did a short daily workout known as the Canadian Air Force exercises, a demanding physical routine.

Another person who attested to Justice Ginsburg's great stamina, physical strength, and enduring resolve was Bryant Johnson, her personal trainer. A military reservist who worked as a federal records clerk during the day, he became personal trainer to a number of judges and justices.

Like her law clerks, Bryant Johnson describes the justice as being tough—"T.A.N. Tough. As. Nails." Justice Ginsburg has credited the one-hour training sessions twice a week with her continued health. Her workout: warming up on the elliptical machine, followed by stretching, balancing with a rubber ball, weight training, and push-ups—reportedly twenty push-ups in two minutes.

The relationship between trainer and client has been described as quite formal. Bryant Johnson has always addressed his client as "Justice," and has never made small talk during her sessions. Which is not to say there was no banter at all. Spotting his client during exercise, Mr. Johnson quipped to her, "Think of the paperwork I'd have to fill out if something happened to you!" Justice Ginsburg remarked appreciatively, "I never thought I'd be able to do any of this. I attribute my well-being to our meetings twice a week. It's essential." She had rarely missed a day on the bench because of illness, despite two bouts with cancer.

Justice Ginsburg being both a lifelong opera lover and passionate about the law, it was perhaps inevitable that her contributions to judicial thinking should end up on the operatic stage.

The composer Derrick Wang recalled that he "probably began scrawling notes on music paper around the age of four, when I was taking piano lessons and thought: Why don't I write my own pieces?" The talented little boy grew into a talented teenager and in high school was scoring plays and conducting musical ensembles. He wrote a musical comedy, which he titled *Prom*. As a college student, he continued to develop his musical skills and talents, but he was not certain that a career in the arts was for him. He applied to law school and not only received his law degree but also found artistic inspiration in the process.

Bryant Johnson, Justice Ginsburg's personal trainer.

Derrick was fascinated by the opposed and competing positions of Justice Ruth Bader Ginsburg, on the liberal side, and Justice Antonin Scalia, on the conservative side. "Every time I read a Scalia dissent," he said, "I would hear music in my head: a rage aria about the Constitution. And when I read the contrasting counterpoint from Justice Ginsburg, I realized: this could be an opera."

A clear distinction between the positions of Justices Scalia and Ginsburg in many of the cases they decided during their tenure on the court had often been remarked on. Justice Scalia became known for his staunchly conservative views on constitutional interpretation, believing that only the text written in 1787 counts and that the document and its meaning do not evolve over time. Justice Ginsburg earned a reputation as a fierce defender of individual rights, believing that the U.S. Constitution is a living document that grows and changes over time as social, cultural, and political shifts occur in society.

Surprisingly, the two justices who frequently opposed each other were close friends, starting when they were Judge Scalia and Judge Ginsburg of the U.S. Court of Appeals for the D.C. Circuit. They served together on that court for six years, until Antonin Scalia was appointed to the U.S. Supreme Court in 1986. Seven years later, Ruth Bader Ginsburg, too, was appointed to the highest court in the land and once again became his colleague. Until Justice Scalia's death in 2016, the deep personal friendship between the two justices remained strong. They often traveled to judicial conferences together and spent downtime being tourists and enjoying the sights. During a visit to India, they took a ride on an elephant together. They and their spouses socialized, spending every New Year's Eve together. "We were best buddies," said Justice Ginsburg after Justice Scalia died.

These two unlikely friends shared a love of opera and frequently went to the opera together. Like Justice Ruth Bader Ginsburg, Justice Scalia was a lifelong opera fan. Unlike her, however, Justice Scalia could sing. He had been in his high school glee club, and as an adult he sang tenor with various choral groups. He had long entertained the fantasy of being a professional musician. Justice Ginsburg dreamed about being a singer and often said, "If I could choose the talent I would most like to have, it would be a glorious voice. I would be a great diva." But, lacking her colleague's true musical talent, she would remind herself that her elementary school music teacher instructed her to mouth the words the chorus was singing, calling her "a sparrow, not a robin."

Justices Ginsburg and Scalia riding an elephant in Jaipur, India.

The two justices were delighted to learn that the recently licensed law-yer Derrick Wang had written a humorous opera based on their words, positions, and surprising friendship, inspired by the two justices' opinions and dissents in his law school days.

Derrick Wang's opera borrowed the musical styles of famous opera composers and placed in the libretto word-for-word quotations from vari-ous opinions (majority or dissenting) of both the justices. In real life, the two of them were more often than not on opposite sides of cases being considered by the court. In the opera, their dueling vocal dialogue is a musical tribute to their two very different ways of seeing and interpreting the Constitution.

The opera's world premiere took place in July 2015. There was a special private pre-premiere event on June 27, 2013, the day after Edie Windsor won her case before the U.S. Supreme Court. Justice Ginsburg and Justice Scalia attended a preview performance of the opera *Scalia/Ginsburg*. Derrick Wang asked for their views and comments, and the two justices, who were very pleased with the opera, were happy to provide their input. Justice Ginsburg believed it contained "an important message brought out in the first duet: 'We are different, we are one'—one in our reverence for the Constitution, the U.S. judiciary, and the Court on which we serve."

A regular opera-goer, Justice Ruth Bader Ginsburg also inaugurated a tradition of presenting two musicales during each term of the court. The audience for these elegant events, held in a beautiful conference room in the Supreme Court building, included all the justices and dozens of friends and family members, who heard some of the world's greatest singers perform classic operatic arias and the like.

While she was never the diva she wished she could have been, Justice Ginsburg's ambition was partially realized when she appeared with the Washington National Opera at the Kennedy Center for the Performing Arts in D.C. in nonspeaking roles in several operas, as Justice Scalia also had during his lifetime. She was onstage for performances of Richard Strauss's *Ariadne auf Naxos* and Johann Strauss II's *Die Fledermaus*. Even more exciting for her, and for her growing cadre of fans, was her appearance in a speaking role in *The Daughter of the Regiment*, an opera by Gaetano Donizetti. For one performance, on November 12, 2016, Ruth Bader Ginsburg was *almost* a diva: She played the Duchess of Krakenthorp, a comedic role. She wrote her own dialogue for her scene and delivered it in English using a body mic. The Duchess of Krakenthorp questioned the character Marie, who was seeking to marry the Duchess's son. As the

Justice Ginsburg backstage at the Washington National Opera, rehearsing her debut speaking role in *The Daughter of the Regiment*.

stern Duchess, Justice Ginsburg delivered a series of searching and sarcastic questions in complete deadpan style, greeted by laughter and applause from the audience.

Justice Ginsburg's obvious fondness for theatrical performance was also displayed when she played the role of a judge in numerous public mock trials, as her fellow Supreme Court justices and judges from other courts traditionally did. Mock trials are most often somewhat tongue-in-cheek performances built around historical or fictional situations of conflict or disagreement. They can involve reenactments of actual trials that occurred in the past, such as the trial of the philosopher Socrates for moral corruption and godlessness. Or they can focus on actual historical events where some sort of injury or criminal action took place but was not judged in court at the time, such as the trial of King Richard III for the murder of his nephews in the Tower of London. Many mock trials are built on events in the plays of William Shakespeare.

In the spring of 2017, Justice Ginsburg was the presiding judge in *The Trial of the Weird Sisters,* hearing arguments supporting and challenging the death sentences for the three witches in Shakespeare's *Macbeth*. She also appeared in mock trials that involved incidents in Shakespeare's *Merchant of Venice,* when Shylock appeals the finding of conspiracy against him; in *Henry IV,* Parts I and II, debating whether Sir John Falstaff should have been compensated for his services to Prince Hal and reinstated as a member of the royal court; in *Othello,* determining whether Iago was guilty of murdering Othello and Desdemona; in *Twelfth Night,* when Malvolio seeks damages for unlawful imprisonment; and in *Much Ado About Nothing,* in the divorce proceedings of Claudio and Lady Hero of Messina. The classic Spanish novel *Don Quixote,* by Miguel Cervantes, supplied an occasion for argument in *The Trial of Don Quixote* to determine whether Don Quixote is insane and requires a guardian. When asked about her participation in mock trials, Justice Ginsburg declared, "I describe it as fun."

Fun, too, were the social events at which Marty interacted with his wife's colleagues and their spouses. There had long been a Supreme Court tradition of spouses' lunches, where the wives of the all-male justices would prepare dishes for the nine couples to enjoy. When Sandra Day O'Connor became the first woman justice to be appointed to the Supreme Court, the wives of the other justices invited Justice O'Connor's husband to join them at the spouses' luncheons, held three times a year. The second male spouse to participate in those traditional events was Marty Ginsburg. His superb cooking skills took the other spouses by surprise, and for a while there was some doubt about whether he himself had really cooked the dish he brought. His talents as a chef were confirmed each time he baked a birthday cake for one of the justices that was obviously not made from a box of cake mix. After Marty's death in 2010, the spouses' group published a collection of his favorite recipes called *Chef Supreme: Martin Ginsburg.*

On the morning of June 28, 2010, in the Supreme Court courtroom, Chief Justice John Roberts somberly stated from the bench: "It is my very sad duty to announce that Martin David Ginsburg, husband of our colleague Justice Ruth Bader Ginsburg, died yesterday . . . at home in Washington, D.C." Justice Ginsburg's husband had died two days after the anniversary of her mother's death in 1950, and four days after the fifty-sixth anniversary of their marriage. Justice Ginsburg's colleagues had heard the news shortly before the public announcement, but everyone else in the courtroom was shocked and saddened.

Many people were probably surprised to see Justice Ginsburg in court on the day after her husband's death. No one who knew her would have expected anything less. In her absence, a colleague could have announced the majority opinion she had been writing during the previous months, but she had asked herself, "What would Marty want me to do?" Marty would have wanted her to be in court, reading her opinion. And so she was in court that day, ready to read.

Justice Ruth Bader Ginsburg's impact on individuals like Sydney Brannoch will never be fully known. The effects of her work in the legal sphere, as a professor and advocate and then as a judge and justice, speak for themselves. Her strategic work in the early part of her career brought about a step-by-step reconfiguration of laws and practices in the United States that had for decades, if not centuries, discriminated against one gender or the other. As Judge Ginsburg and Justice Ginsburg, she continued, through

Justice Ginsburg poses with Marty, her chef supreme, in work clothes.
She is in judicial robe with frilly jabot; he wears his typical cooking outfit,
shorts and a French cook's apron. Photograph by Mariana Cook

her opinions, to affect the ways in which the U.S. Constitution is interpreted in areas that deeply affect ordinary citizens. And the future may see Justice Ginsburg's dissenting opinions in critical areas of constitutional interpretation become majority positions written into law by Congress.

Justice Ruth Bader Ginsburg's life and work were dedicated to fairness and equality, to the rights of all Americans. Her hard work, persistence, and unstinting devotion to the cause of justice will continue to leave their mark on the lives of all citizens. Particularly powerful in her unrelenting push for equal rights is her view of the nation's most significant document, one that she views as living and as constantly changing: "The genius of our Constitution," she said in February 2018, "is that this concept of 'We the people' has become ever more embracive." Our Constitution "is still being perfected but is ever more inclusive."

ACKNOWLEDGMENTS

I would like to thank my subject, Justice Ruth Bader Ginsburg, for her interest in and enthusiasm for my project. She was gracious in responding to my questions promptly and fully and generous in sharing information and photographs with me. She kindly asked Lauren Brewer, her assistant, to arrange for reserved seats for me during three mornings of oral argument at the Supreme Court. For all of this I am deeply grateful.

It would have been difficult for me to move smoothly through the research and writing of this book without the constant support of my wife, Jennifer Elrod. She was an expert researcher, a just critic of early drafts, and a perfect sounding board for thoughts and ideas about the content and organization of the book.

I very much appreciate the insights into Justice Ginsburg's early years from Sandy Goldberg Roche, a classmate of hers and, in a remarkable coincidence, a former colleague of mine. She and a few other elementary school classmates of the Justice willingly shared their memories of "Kiki" when she was with them at PS 238.

I am lucky to have known, during my years as dean of students at the University of California, Berkeley, School of Law, a number of Justice Ginsburg's former law clerks, all of them now lawyers and/or law professors. I am indebted to Neil Siegel, Linda Lye, and Heather Elliott for sharing their memories of and insights into their clerkships with the Justice. The details they were able to provide about the experience of working with Justice Ginsburg were tremendously helpful. I also had the privilege of knowing the late Herma Hill Kay, former dean and law professor. She was tremendously helpful in sharing views about her work with Ruth Bader Ginsburg in creating the first law casebook to address gender discrimination.

I am so happy that I was able to communicate with several of the heroes of the legal stories I tell in the book. Sharron (Frontiero) Cohen, Curtis Craig, Lindsay Earls, Savana Redding, and Stephen Wiesenfeld were all responsive and more than willing to share details about having been parties in lawsuits that grew out of often painful situations they faced as ordinary citizens pursuing their rights in court. Their contributions allowed me to build my chapters around their personal stories.

Sydney Brannoch, entomologist supreme, gave me a very thoughtful account of her life and her special way of honoring Justice Ginsburg. She is by no means the only person whose life and professional paths have been deeply influenced by the life and work of Justice Ginsburg.

Thanks to the attorneys who represented parties in cases that came before either Judge or Justice Ginsburg, in particular Robert Kapp, who was one of Inez Wright's attorneys in her lawsuit against the tax breaks given to segregated schools in Memphis, Tennessee. My gratitude, too, to attorneys Michael Banks, David Goldberg, Leo Martinez, and Dan Ortiz, who shared with me recollections of cases that are not discussed in this book but were important to the development of Justice Ginsburg's jurisprudence.

Many professional librarians and researchers have contributed their efforts in support of this book. My deepest gratitude goes to Dean Rowan, Reference Librarian at Berkeley Law (and a former student of mine!). He was tireless in hunting down hard-to-find materials and in sharing ideas about the law in general and Justice Ginsburg in particular. Without him, my research efforts would have been much more arduous. I would also like to thank William Benemann, Berkeley Law archivist emeritus, for his assistance.

Jeffrey Flannery and his staff always had the correct boxes of Ruth Bader Ginsburg papers ready for me during the days I spent researching at the Library of Congress. They answered all my questions and made for an extremely positive and productive visit.

Thanks to the many people who provided photographs that appear in this book: Savana Redding, Lindsay Earls, Sharron Cohen, Stephen Wiesenfeld, Sydney Brannoch, Jim Block, Franz Jantzen and Fred Schilling of the Supreme Court, personal trainer Bryant Johnson, attorney Roberta Kaplan, and Michael Klinger and Deborah Cheng who went to Brooklyn to take photos of the house where the Justice was raised.

Lastly, I would like to express my deepest gratitude to my editor supreme, Dinah Stevenson. Her expertise and skillful editing, her creativity and clarity, have all had a deep impact on the shaping of this work.

APPENDIX I:
THE BILL OF RIGHTS

AMENDMENT I

Congress shall make no law respecting an establishment of religion, or prohibiting the free exercise thereof; or abridging the freedom of speech, or of the press; or the right of the people peaceably to assemble, and to petition the government for a redress of grievances.

AMENDMENT II

A well regulated militia, being necessary to the security of a free state, the right of the people to keep and bear arms, shall not be infringed.

AMENDMENT III

No soldier shall, in time of peace be quartered in any house, without the consent of the owner, nor in time of war, but in a manner to be prescribed by law.

AMENDMENT IV

The right of the people to be secure in their persons, houses, papers, and effects, against unreasonable searches and seizures, shall not be violated, and no warrants shall issue, but upon probable cause, supported by oath or affirmation, and particularly describing the place to be searched, and the persons or things to be seized.

AMENDMENT V

No person shall be held to answer for a capital, or otherwise infamous crime, unless on a presentment or indictment of a grand jury, except in cases arising in the land or naval forces, or in the militia, when in actual service in time of war or public danger;

nor shall any person be subject for the same offense to be twice put in jeopardy of life or limb; nor shall be compelled in any criminal case to be a witness against himself, nor be deprived of life, liberty, or property, without due process of law; nor shall private property be taken for public use, without just compensation.

AMENDMENT VI

In all criminal prosecutions, the accused shall enjoy the right to a speedy and public trial, by an impartial jury of the state and district wherein the crime shall have been committed, which district shall have been previously ascertained by law, and to be informed of the nature and cause of the accusation; to be confronted with the witnesses against him; to have compulsory process for obtaining witnesses in his favor, and to have the assistance of counsel for his defense.

AMENDMENT VII

In suits at common law, where the value in controversy shall exceed twenty dollars, the right of trial by jury shall be preserved, and no fact tried by a jury, shall be otherwise reexamined in any court of the United States, than according to the rules of the common law.

AMENDMENT VIII

Excessive bail shall not be required, nor excessive fines imposed, nor cruel and unusual punishments inflicted.

AMENDMENT IX

The enumeration in the Constitution, of certain rights, shall not be construed to deny or disparage others retained by the people.

AMENDMENT X

The powers not delegated to the United States by the Constitution, nor prohibited by it to the states, are reserved to the states respectively, or to the people.

APPENDIX II:
SOME IMPORTANT ADDITIONAL DISSENTS WRITTEN OR JOINED BY JUSTICE RUTH BADER GINSBURG

Names of specific cases are followed by their official case citations. These indicate in a kind of shorthand the court where the decision was handed down, where it is published, in which volume and on what page is appears, and the publication year.

COURT OF APPEALS—DISSENTING OPINION

Goldman v. Secretary of Defense, 739 F2d 657 (D.C. Cir. 1984)—The District Court would not rehear a case involving a Jewish military officer and doctor who was not permitted to wear a yarmulke while on duty. Judge Ginsburg noted that Dr. Goldman "has long served his country as an Air Force officer with honor and devotion." His commander's deeming Dr. Goldman's wearing his yarmulke "intolerable . . . runs counter to the best of our traditions to accommodate . . . the spiritual needs of our people."

SUPREME COURT—DISSENTING OPINIONS

Bush v. Gore, 531 US 98 (2000)
In the 2000 presidential election, the two candidates were Republican George W. Bush and Democrat Al Gore. The popular vote in Florida was so close that a recount was ordered by that state's highest court. But it was challenged, and the issue was finally reached the U.S. Supreme Court. There, the majority held that Florida's method of recounting the presidential election ballots was unconstitutional. This effectively made George W. Bush the president, though he lost the election in the popular vote. Justice Ginsburg joined three of her colleagues in a dissenting opinion, believing that the decision of the Florida Supreme Court should have been honored and not overturned.

Gratz v. Bollinger, 539 US 244 (2003)

The University of Michigan, like many other such institutions, looked at various factors in deciding whether or not to admit students to their school, including the race of the applicant. In the Supreme Court, the majority held that the University of Michigan's admissions practices were unconstitutional where they took the race of college applicants into account. In her dissenting opinion, Justice Ginsburg wrote that the university was not in violation of the Equal Protection Clause of the U.S. Constitution in considering race as one of many factors because there was no quota by race and no special seats reserved for people of particular races. "The stain of generations of racial oppression is still visible in our society," she wrote.

Citizens United v. FEC, 558 US 310 (2010)

The majority held that political spending is a form of protected speech under the First Amendment to the Constitution. Therefore, the government may not prevent corporations or unions or other associations from spending money to support or denounce individual candidates in elections. Justice Ginsburg joined three of her colleagues in dissenting. The Justice continued to express publicly that this was a ruling she would like to see overruled. "I think the notion that we have all the democracy that money can buy strays so far from what our democracy was supposed to be," she said.

Burwell v. Hobby Lobby (2014)

A corporation sued in order to be free from complying with certain regulations involving the funding of medical services for women employees, claiming that compliance was against the religious beliefs of the corporation's owners. In the Supreme Court, the majority held that it was lawful for certain for-profit corporations to be exempt from a law or regulation if the owners objected to it on religious grounds. Justice Ginsburg attacked the majority opinion for essentially giving corporations the right to not comply with any law they choose, for "religious" reasons. She believed that corporations should not be treated as if they are people, entitled to certain rights and protections, but should be challenged for infringing the rights of individuals they employ.

APPENDIX III:
STRUCTURE OF
THE FEDERAL COURT SYSTEM

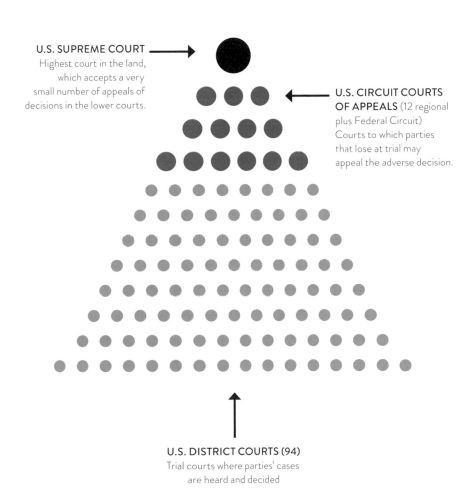

U.S. SUPREME COURT
Highest court in the land,
which accepts a very
small number of appeals of
decisions in the lower courts.

**U.S. CIRCUIT COURTS
OF APPEALS** (12 regional
plus Federal Circuit)
Courts to which parties
that lose at trial may
appeal the adverse decision.

U.S. DISTRICT COURTS (94)
Trial courts where parties' cases
are heard and decided

NOTES

ONE: A Teen Takes Her Case to the Supreme Court

1   *"Ever since I was little . . . miss a day of it"*: Savana Redding in videotaped interview for the ACLU (aclu.org/video/savana-redding-her-supreme-court-case; accessed March 1, 2017).

2   *"I didn't have an option . . . it would be handled"*: "Justices Hear School Strip-Search Arguments," NBC News, April 21, 2009 (www.nbcnews.com/id/30295244/ns/us_news-crime_ and_courts/t/justices-hear-school-strip-search-arguments/#.Wg3cuLaZOi4; accessed April 18, 2017).

     "Then they asked me to . . . was about to cry": Savana Redding's affidavit, November 3, 2004, p. 3 (www.aclu.org/legal-document/redding-v-safford-affidavit-savana-redding; accessed April 22, 2017).

3   *"When Savana came out . . . Crying"*: April Redding, Savana Redding's mother, in videotaped interview for ACLU (www.aclu.org/video/savana-redding-her-supreme-court-case; accessed March 1, 2017).

     "School had always been . . . by the teachers": Savana Redding to the author via Facebook, December 9, 2016.

4   *"It's more about other . . . Ever"*: Savana Redding in videotaped interview for the ACLU (www.aclu.org/videos/savana-redding-her-supreme-court-case; accessed March 1, 2017).

6   *"overwhelming"*: Savana Redding to the author via Facebook, December 9, 2016.

7   *"The Honorable, the Chief Justice . . . Honorable Court!"*: Announcement by the marshal of the court at the beginning of each session of the United States Supreme Court. Everyone in the courtroom must stand and may sit down only after the justices have been seated (www.supremecourt.gov/about/procedures.aspx; accessed April 22, 2018).

13   *"In the third grade I brought home . . . earn an 'A'"*: L. C. Pogrebin, "The Working Woman," p. 34.

[13] *"One of my most pleasant . . . to me"*: Bucklo, "Rules to Live By," p. 8.

[14] *"Nancy was a girl who did things . . . than she was"*: R. B. Ginsburg, *My Own Words*, p. 5.

    "was a girl . . . be wallflowers": Academy of Achievement, "Pioneer of Gender Equality."

[15] *"We children of public school age . . . everlasting peace"*: R. B. Ginsburg, *My Own Words*, pp. 10–11.

    "Nobody wanted to believe what was really happening": R. B. Ginsburg, *My Own Words*, p. 6.

[16] *"One could not help . . . in our world"*: Ruth Bader Ginsburg speech at the Holocaust Museum, *Voices on Antisemitism* podcast, November 9, 2006 (www.ushmm.org/confront-antisemitism/antisemitism-podcast/ruth-bader-ginsburg-voa; accessed November 4, 2016).

    "I have memories . . . 'allowed' ": Ruth Bader Ginsburg testimony at Confirmation Hearings Before the Committee on the Judiciary, United States Senate, July 20, 1993, p. 139.

    "never to forget . . . camps": R. B. Ginsburg, *My Own Words*, p. 16.

    "No one can feel free . . . together again": R. B. Ginsburg, *My Own Words*, p. 16.

[17] *"experience nature . . . expectations"*: Camps Baco and Che-Na-Wah website; accessed July 3, 2016).

[18] *"while I can still paddle my own canoe"*: Bayer, *Ruth Bader Ginsburg*, p. 24.

[21] *"My lawyers had advised . . . see past that"*: Savana Redding to the author via Facebook, December 9, 2016.

    "There were jokes . . . well-taken": Academy of Achievement, "Pioneer of Gender Equality."

[22] *"would talk some sense . . . locker room"*: Savana Redding to the author via Facebook, December 9, 2016.

[23] *"abusive and it was not . . .permitted it"*: Ruth Bader Ginsburg, Concurring Opinion, *Safford Unified School District #1 v. Redding*, June 25, 2009.

"She helped restore . . . system": Savana Redding to the author via Facebook, December 9, 2016.

"They have never been . . . quite understand": Biskupic, "Ginsburg: Court Needs Another Woman."

TWO: STUDENTS HAVE RIGHTS TOO

24 *"goody two-shoes"*: "Lindsay Earls, American Heroine," *Native American Netroots,* July 23, 2010 (nativeamericannetroots.net/diary/595; accessed October 17, 2016).

25 *"the normal sounds of urination"*: Brief of the Respondents, *Board of Education of Independent School Dist. #92 of Pottawatomie County v. Earls*, February 6, 2002.

   "to ensure that it was . . . color and clarity": Brief of the Respondents, *Board of Education of Independent School Dist. #92 of Pottawatomie County v. Earls*, February 6, 2002.

26 *"It was such . . . life"*: Lindsay Earls, email to author, October 19, 2016.

   "Afterwards, a group of kids . . . I believed in": Lindsay Earls, email to author, October 19, 2016.

27 *"She made me toe . . . her disappointment"*: Galanes, "Ruth Bader Ginsburg and Gloria Steinem"

   "It was one of the most . . . that's what I did": Lamb, "Justice Ruth Bader Ginsburg," p. 113.

   "[Ruth] was always prepared . . . according to height!": Sandra Goldberg Roche, email to author, June 19, 2016.

28 *"She was very modest . . . aced them"*: Margolick, "Trial by Adversity Shapes Jurist Outlook."

   "I read books . . . in the curriculum": Ruth Bader Ginsburg, letter to the author, June 7, 2017.

29 *"the bravest . . . known"*: Ruth Bader Ginsburg, remarks on the occasion of her nomination to the Supreme Court by President Bill Clinton, June 14, 1993.

29   *"My mother influenced . . . resourceful"*: Vrato, *The Counselors*, p. 175.

      "the house was filled . . . in the minyan": A. Pogrebin, "In Chambers with Ruth Bader Ginsburg," p. 33.

30   *"My mother had mixed . . . to pieces"*: A. Pogrebin, *Stars of David*, p. 23.

      "I was seventeen . . . behind the man": L. C. Pogrebin, "The Working Woman," p. 34.

31   *"My mother never . . . less of a man"*: L. C. Pogrebin, "The Working Woman," p. 34.

      "playing [cello] . . . Robinson": Toohey, "Brooklyn School's Many Famous Alumni."

      "stuck up": Bayer, *Ruth Bader Ginsburg*, p. 23.

      "magnetism that drew people to her": Bayer, *Ruth Bader Ginsburg*, p. 23.

32   *"Ruth wouldn't speak . . . on her mind"*: Bayer, *Ruth Bader Ginsburg*, p. 23.

      "Ruth came to all . . . ball players": Sandra Goldberg Roche, email to author, June 19, 2016.

      "So you're going . . . chicken flicker": Sandra Goldberg Roche, email to author, June 19, 2016. Chicken flickers were women who pulled the feathers off chickens in local butcher shops.

35   *"The best part . . . questions"*: Ruth Bader Ginsburg in "Ruth Bader Ginsburg: Humble. Pursuits." Behrman House (www.behrmanhouse.com/RL/justice-ruth-bader-ginsburg-humble-pursuits; accessed July 12, 2016).

38   *"I thought he was . . . my case!"*: Lindsay Earls, email to author, October 19, 2016.

      "not reasonable . . . capricious, even perverse": Ruth Bader Ginsburg, Dissenting Opinion, *Pottawatomie v. Earls*, June 27, 2002.

      "Justice Ginsburg's dissent . . . just a kid": Lindsay Earls, email to author, October 19, 2016.

THREE: Standing Up for Free Expression

40   *"a kid who liked to push buttons"*: Tom Kizzia, "'Bong Hits 4 Jesus' Goes to the Supreme Court," *Anchorage Daily News,* March 4, 2007 (www.november.org/stayinfo/breaking07/BongHits.html; accessed April 29, 2017).

"would clearly be . . . administration": Frederick, "Joe's Story."

41 *"in front of the entire nation!"*: Frederick, "Joe's Story."

"This was the protected speech . . . by CNN": Frederick, "Joe's Story."

42 *"thought it was dumb"*: Kizzia, "'Bong Hits 4 Jesus' Goes to the Supreme Court."

"What about my . . . do not have free speech": Frederick, "Joe's Story."

"People were mostly . . . backup": Kizzia, "'Bong Hits 4 Jesus' Goes to the Supreme Court."

43 *"Students do not shed . . . gate"*: Majority Opinion, *Tinker v. Des Moines,* February 24, 1969.

44 *"It could have been . . . the others"*: Alumni Affairs, "Ruth Bader Ginsburg."

"The thing to do was to be a party girl": Goldberg, "The Second Woman Justice," p. 48.

"Study hard . . . buried": Ayer, "Ruth Bader Ginsburg." p. 20.

45 *"a pleasant but undistinguished evening"*: Bayer, *Ruth Bader Ginsburg,* p. 29.

46 *"He was a man in love . . . way I write"*: Garner, "Ruth Bader Ginsburg," p. 135.

"a magnificent depository . . . social": Linda Myers, "Milton R. Konvitz: Cornell Memorial Statement, March 12, 1908–September 5, 2003." ILR School, Cornell University, September 8, 2003 (www.ilr.cornell.edu/about-ilr/founding-faculty/milton-r-konvitz; accessed August 13, 2017).

47 *"In his gentle way . . . as I could"*: Garner, "Ruth Bader Ginsburg," p. 135.

"Get it right . . . decorations": R. B. Ginsburg, "Remarks for the American Law Institute Annual Dinner."

50 *"Professor Cushman wanted . . . speak or write"*: Academy of Achievement, "Pioneer of Gender Equality."

51 *"I am prepared to talk freely . . . associates"*: Professor Marcus Singer, Testimony at the Hearings of the House Un-American Activities Committee, May 26, 1953, p. 1554.

52 *"to be in the same discipline . . . was doing"*: Mathews, "The Spouse of Ruth."

"That a lawyer could do . . . for me": Bayer, *Ruth Bader Ginsburg,* pp. 27–29.

52 *"I stood very low in my class!"*: Martin Ginsburg, informal biographical note at his law firm, as quoted in "The 'Histories' of the Cornell Class of '54," compiled and edited by Robert Frederic Martin, Class Historian (cornelluniversity.imodules.com/s/1717/images/gid5/editor_documents/1954_folder_/54_websitehistory-3—jk.pdf; accessed April 26, 2016).

53 *"scary smart"*: Margolick, "Trial by Adversity Shapes Jurist's Outlook."

"the most important . . . M.R.S.": ACLU, "Tribute."

"was the school for parents . . . hopeless": Galanes, "Ruth Bader Ginsburg and Gloria Steinem."

54 *"there were lawyers . . . committees"*: Alumni Affairs, "Ruth Bader Ginsburg."

55 *"[the students] were released . . . assembly"*: Ruth Bader Ginsburg, Oral Argument in *Morse v. Frederick*, March 19, 2007, pp. 27–28.

"This is a nonsense message, not advocacy": Dissenting Opinion, *Morse v. Frederick*, June 25, 2007, p. 49.

FOUR: MARRIAGE RIGHTS, PAST AND PRESENT

57 *"In a perfect world . . . luxury"*: "Jim Obergefell," *Biography* (www.biography.com/people/jim-obergefell; accessed May 14, 2007).

Same-Sex Marriage: Legal marriage between two people of the same sex or gender was becoming more and more common as the twentieth century ended. Increasingly, throughout the world, it was deemed simply unfair and unjust for a whole category of people to be unable to receive the benefits of a legally recognized marriage. In 2001, the Netherlands passed the first law allowing for two women or two men to marry. In the decade or more that followed, almost two dozen countries followed suit. In the United States, the movement for marriage equality, as it came to be known, became particularly serious in the early 1990s; by the early 2000s, legal actions in counties, states, and at the federal level led eventually to more and more states allowing same-sex couples to marry.

63 *"as close to inedible as food could be"*: Carlson, "The Law According to Ruth," p. 38.

"were not considered worth documenting": Von Drehle, "Conventional Roles Hid a Revolutionary Intellect."

64   *"If you want to be . . . a way"*: Gluck, "A Conversation with Justice Ruth Bader Ginsburg," p. 21.

"We want to find . . . children": "The 'Histories' of the Cornell Class of '54," compiled and edited by Robert Frederic Martin, Class Historian (cornelluniversity.imodules.com/s/1717/images/gid5/editor_documents/1954_folder_/54_websitehistory-3—jk.pdf; accessed April 26, 2016).

"a relationship of . . . female": Ruth Bader Ginsburg, Oral Argument, *Obergefell v. Hodges*, April 28, 2015.

65   *"Marty was . . . the other"*: Carmon, "Exclusive Justice Ruth Bader Ginsburg Interview."

66   *"My dear Marty . . . threat"*: Tassler, *What I Told My Daughter*, p. 113.

FIVE: WOMEN WORKING IN "A MAN'S WORLD"

68   *"I was brought up an only child . . . people"*: Sarfati, "Lilly Ledbetter, the Woman Behind the Fair Pay Act."

"dream job": Lilly Ledbetter, The Lilly Ledbetter Fair Pay Act (www.lillyledbetter.com.index.html; accessed December 12, 2016).

69   *"It's like coaching . . . inventory"*: Frauenheim, "Lilly Ledbetter Interview."

"That showed respect": Frauenheim, "Lilly Ledbetter Interview."

"By the time I realized . . . overtime": Sarfati, "Ledbetter, the Woman Behind the Fair Pay Act."

"little torn sheet of paper": "What Lilly Ledbetter Wants Women to Know About Equal Pay."

70   *"I was just humiliated . . . that way"*: "What Lilly Ledbetter Wants Women to Know About Equal Pay."

71   *"I was so embarrassed . . . husband's work"*: Galanes, "Ruth Bader Ginsburg and Gloria Steinem."

74   *"Employers would post . . . things were"*: Bucklo, "Rules to Live By," p. 10.

Paul, Weiss: Coincidentally, this was the same firm—Paul, Weiss, Rifkind, Wharton and Garrison—that decades earlier had neglected to offer the new law school graduate Ruth Bader Ginsburg a position as a full-time associate!

"I thought I had done . . . graduation": Swiger, "Ruth Bader Ginsburg," p. 58.

77   *"shows the differences between . . . that way"*: Academy of Achievement, "Pioneer of Gender Equality."

78   *"Why should the woman . . . only one?"*: Merritt and Williams, "Transcript of Interview of U.S. Supreme Court Associate Justice Ruth Bader Ginsburg" (Ruth Bader Ginsburg quoting Eva Moberg), p. 806.

79   *"very meticulous . . . right"*: Von Drehle, "Conventional Roles Hid a Revolutionary Intellect."

"I loved to hear . . . the text": Von Drehle, "Conventional Roles Hid a Revolutionary Intellect."

"I repaired to the library . . . months' time": Kay, "Claiming a Space in the Law School Curriculum," p. 55.

"I was teaching procedure . . . civil liberties": Harrington, *Women Lawyers,* p. 208.

85   *"None of those cases are ever solved overnight"*: "What Lilly Ledbetter Wants Women to Know About Equal Pay."

86   *"was one that every woman . . . didn't"*: Epstein, "Ruth Bader Ginsburg."

87   *"Ledbetter was . . . victory"*: Epstein, "Ruth Bader Ginsburg."

SIX: PROTECTING ALL CAREGIVERS

90   *"I went next door . . . And we did"*: M. D. Ginsburg, "A Uniquely Distinguished Service," p. 173.

92   *"His classmates . . . exams"*: Academy of Achievement, "Pioneer of Gender Equality."

"Because of the radiation . . . next day": Academy of Achievement, "Pioneer of Gender Equality."

"Frankly we didn't know . . . Jane": Ward, "Family Ties."

94   *"dream for society . . . their kids"*: Von Drehle, "Redefining Fair with a Simple Careful Assault."

Weinberger v. Wiesenfeld: Caspar Weinberger was the Secretary of Health, Education, and Welfare and the representative of the government that Stephen Wiesenfeld was suing.

96   *"Not unlike Martin Ginsburg . . . lifestyles"*: Stephen Wiesenfeld Testimony, Nomination Hearings, July 23, 1993.

"the second love of his life": Rosen, "Ruth Bader Ginsburg Is an American Hero."

SEVEN: STRENGTHENING THE FAMILY UNIT

98   *"I got mixed up in the wrong crowd"*: O'Neill, "Not Going Quietly."

101   *"By the time [Jane] went . . . books"*: R. B. Ginsburg, "Independence," p. 115.

"We dashed her to . . . this day": R. B. Ginsburg, "Independence, p. 115.

"Mommy does . . . the cooking": James Ginsburg in *Chef Supreme: Martin Ginsburg,* Supreme Court Historical Society, 2011, p. 93.

"I remember a friend . . . or something": Ward, "Family Ties."

"somewhat austere . . . in me": Saline and Wohlmuth, *Mothers and Daughters,* p. 50.

102   *"I never thought . . . worked"*: Saline and Wohlmuth, *Mothers and Daughters,* p. 51.

104   *"For instance . . . up with"*: Ward, "Family Ties."

105   *"The family was always home for dinner"*: Hewitt, "Feeling Supreme."

106   *"lively"*: "A Conversation Between Justice Ruth Bader Ginsburg and Professor Robert A. Stein," p. 2.

106   *"even when he was kindergarten age"*: "A Conversation Between Justice Ruth Bader Ginsburg and Professor Robert A. Stein," p. 2.

      "When we first saw James . . . the lye": Swiger, "Ruth Bader Ginsburg," p. 59.

      "pranks": Ward, "Family Ties."

      "a night owl who worked . . . to bed": Campbell and Harrington, "Judge Ruth Bader Ginsburg."

107   *"She was always there . . . didn't"*: Hewitt, "Feeling Supreme."

108   *"Atticus Finch with a laptop"*: Bacon, "Atticus Finch with a Laptop."

      "If it's something . . . take it on": Bacon, "Atticus Finch with a Laptop."

110   *"My client is no longer . . . Mississippi law"*: Robert B. McDuff, Oral Argument, *M.L.B. v. S.L.J.,* October 7, 1996, p. 1.

      "This isn't . . . about money": Ruth Bader Ginsburg, Oral Argument, *M.L.B. v. S.L.J.,* October 7, 1996, p. 36.

111   *"This case concerns . . . parent"*: Ruth Bader Ginsburg, Majority Opinion Announcement, *M.L.B. v. S.L.J.,* December 16, 1996.

      "Mississippi may not deny . . . parent": Ruth Bader Ginsburg, Majority Opinion Announcement, *M.L.B. v. S.L.J.,* December 16, 1996.

      "This is a grand . . . long time": David G. Savage, "Free Parental-Rights Appeal Ordered by Supreme Court," *Los Angeles Times,* December 17, 1996 (articles.latimes.com/1996-12-17/news/mn-9983_1_supreme-court; accessed January 12, 2017).

EIGHT: DEFENDING HARD-WON CIVIL RIGHTS

115   *"stigmatizes black schoolchildren . . . black race"*: Ruth Bader Ginsburg, Majority Opinion, *Wright v. Regan,* June 18, 1981.

      "It's OK to have . . . segregated schools": Inez Wright, *The Tennessean,* Nashville, Tennessee, July 5, 1984, p 9.

116   *"[Dixon] never was able to make . . . appreciated"*: Burritt, "Justice Ginsburg to Speak on Two Great Passions."

   "[as] an African-American . . . Metropolitan Opera": R. B. Ginsburg, "My First Opera."

117   *"a war in which people . . . their race"*: Ruth Bader Ginsburg, Testimony, Confirmation Hearings, July 20, 1993.

   "You felt that every eye . . . curiosity": Bazelon, "The Place of Women on the Court."

   "At Columbia . . . either of them": Bazelon, "The Place of Women on the Court."

118   *"I had three strikes . . . by then"*: Galanes, "Ruth Bader Ginsburg and Gloria Steinem on the Unending Fight for Women's Rights."

   "It seemed inevitable . . . successful strategy": R. B. Ginsburg, "A Conversation with Ruth Bader Ginsburg, Associate Justice of the United States Supreme Court."

   "His life was on the line . . . danger": R. B. Ginsburg, "A Conversation with Ruth Bader Ginsburg, Associate Justice of the United States Supreme Court."

   "how wrong it is . . . skin": Carmon, "Exclusive Justice Ruth Bader Ginsburg Interview."

120   *"There were no big names . . . Selma"*: Lewis, *Walking . . .* , p. 338.

123   *"The sad irony . . . errs egregiously"*: Ruth Bader Ginsburg, Dissenting Opinion, *Shelby County, Alabama v. Eric H. Holder,* June 25, 2013.

   "The Supreme Court has stuck . . . register to vote": Press Release, Congressman Lewis's Office, June 25, 2013.

NINE: WOMEN'S RIGHTS ARE HUMAN RIGHTS

127   *"I am supposed to get . . . qualified!"*: Nora Simon, letter to ACLU, quoted by Ruth Bader Ginsburg in a letter to the Director of Equal Opportunity for the Armed Forces, July 29, 1970, Ruth Bader Ginsburg Papers, Library of Congress, accessed March 27, 2017.

   "I am fully ready to go to court": Nora Simon, letter to the ACLU office in Washington, January 8, 1970, Ruth Bader Ginsburg Papers, Box 7, ACLU File, accessed March 28, 2017.

128   *"preference to members of . . . Fourteenth Amendment"*: Unanimous Opinion, *Reed v. Reed*, November 22, 1971.

129   *"the most powerful person . . . career-oriented person"*: Sharron Frontiero Cohen, notes prepared for a student's PhD dissertation and shared with the author on January 26, 2017.

130   *"I had people telling me . . . I got mad!"*: Mayeri, " 'When the Trouble Started.' "

132   *"I was terribly nervous . . . throw up"*: Swiger, "Ruth Bader Ginsburg," p. 52.

       "Two minutes into . . . carried me through": Swiger, "Ruth Bader Ginsburg," p. 52.

133   *"I ask no favor . . . off our necks"*: Ruth Bader Ginsburg, Oral Argument, *Frontiero v. Richardson*, May 14, 1973.

136   *"all look like me"*: Academy of Achievement, "Pioneer of Gender Equality."

137   *"because in the days . . . judge"*: Academy of Achievement, "Pioneer of Gender Equality."

141   *"an opportunity beyond . . . a judge"*: Ruth Bader Ginsburg, Testimony, Confirmation Hearings, July 20, 1993.

142   *"can constitutionally deny . . . uniquely affords"*: Ruth Bader Ginsburg, Majority Opinion, *U.S. v. VMI*, June 26, 1996.

143   *"This should be Ruth's"*: Hirshman, *Sisters in Law,* p. xii.

       "I have thought of you . . . afraid to complain": Ruth Bader Ginsburg to Nora Simon Hanke, December 28, 1973, Ruth Bader Ginsburg Papers, Library of Congress, accessed March 28, 2017.

TEN: BLAZING A TRAIL, LEAVING HER MARK

145   *"Early childhood exposure . . . many directions"*: Sydney K. Brannoch, email to author, July 1, 2017.

       "book after book": Sydney K. Brannoch, email to author, July 1, 2017.

       "took an entomology class . . . diversity of insects": Sydney K. Brannoch, email to author, July 1, 2017.

147   *"Without Ruth Bader Ginsburg . . . freely"*: Sydney K. Brannoch, email to author, July 1, 2017.

"why female specimens . . . most species": Sydney Brannoch, "Insect Named for Ruth Bader Ginsburg Is Step Toward Equality of the 6-Legged Sexes," NPR-America, June 2, 2016 (www.npr.org/sections/thetwo-way/2016/06/02/480437128/insect-named-for-ruth-bader-ginsburg-is-step-toward-equality-of-the-6-legged-sex; accessed July 1, 2017).

148   *"sap energy . . . endeavors"*: Thomas, "The Honorable Ruth Bader Ginsburg," p. 116.

149   *"She trained me well . . . language matters"*: Neil Siegel, now a professor at Duke University Law School, telephone conversation with author, July 12, 2017.

150   *"an amazing presence . . . your career"*: Schlanger, "Five Former Clerks Share Thoughts About Justices Ginsburg."

"it's always about the case, not about egos": Neil Siegel, now a professor at Duke University Law School, telephone conversation with author, July 12, 2017.

"command of the big picture . . . detail": Linda Lye, now senior staff attorney, ACLU Foundation of Northern California, email to author, July 26, 2017.

"smart, diligent . . . human beings": Linda Lye, now senior staff attorney, ACLU Foundation of Northern California, email to author, July 26, 2017.

151   *"generous and supportive . . . my daughters' lives"*: Neil Siegel, now a professor at Duke University Law School, telephone conversation with author, July 12, 2017.

152   *"T.A.N. Tough. As. Nails"*: Cole, "The Man Who Builds the Bodies of the Law."

"Think of the paperwork . . . to you": Halper, "Justice Ginsburg on Working Out."

"I never thought I'd be . . . essential": Halper, "Justice Ginsburg on Working Out."

153   *"probably began scrawling . . . pieces"*: Derrick Wang, interviewed by D. Dona Le, July 1, 2017.

"Every time I read . . . an opera": Derrick Wang, interviewed by D. Dona Le, July 1, 2017, *Harvardwood* (www.harvardwood.org/watn_derrick_wang; accessed July 15, 2017).

154   *"We were best buddies"*: NPR Staff, "Ginsburg and Scalia."

154   *"If I could choose . . . great diva"*: R. B. Ginsburg, "Prefaces to *Scalia/Ginsburg*."

"a sparrow, not a robin": R. B. Ginsburg, "A Conversation with Ruth Bader Ginsburg, Associate Justice of the United States Supreme Court," p. 2.

156   *"an important message . . . we serve"*: R. B. Ginsburg, "Prefaces to *Scalia/Ginsburg*."

158   *"I describe it as fun"*: Donadio, "Justice Ruth Bader Ginsburg Presides Over Shylock's Appeal."

159   *"It is my very sad duty . . . Washington, D.C."*: Chief Justice Roberts, Public Statement, June 28, 2010.

"What would Marty want me to do?": Academy of Achievement, "Pioneer of Gender Equality."

161   *"The genius of our Constitution . . . more inclusive"*: Boorstein, "Ruth Bader Ginsburg Calls for Equal Rights Amendment to the Constitution."

BIBLIOGRAPHY

"A Conversation Between Justice Ruth Bader Ginsburg and Professor Robert A. Stein." *Minnesota Law Review* 99 (November 3, 2014): 1–25.

Academy of Achievement. "Pioneer of Gender Equality." Interviews of Ruth Bader Ginsburg on August 17, 2010, and July 14, 2016. www.achievement.org/achiever/ruth-bader-ginsburg/#interview. Accessed 2016–2017.

ACLU. "Tribute: The Legacy of Ruth Bader Ginsburg and WRP Staff." 2015. www.aclu.org/other/tribute-legacy-ruth-bader-ginsburg-and-wrp-staff. Accessed October 5, 2016.

Alumni Affairs. "Ruth Bader Ginsburg: From Brooklyn to the Bench." Cornellcast. College of Arts and Sciences. Cornell University. September 22, 2014. www.cornell.edu/video/ruth-bader-ginsburg-brooklyn-to-the-bench. Accessed April 17, 2017.

Ayer, Eleanor H. *Ruth Bader Ginsburg: Fire and Steel on the Supreme Court.* New York: Dillon Press, 1994.

Bacon, Katie. "Atticus Finch with a Laptop." *Harvard Law Bulletin,* Summer 2012. today.law.harvard.edu/atticus-finch-with-a-laptop. Accessed December 20, 2016.

Bayer, Linda. *Ruth Bader Ginsburg.* New York: Chelsea House Publishers, 2000.

Bazelon, Emily. "The Place of Women on the Court." *New York Times Magazine,* July 7, 2009. www.nytimes.com/2009/07/12/magazine/12ginsburg-t.html. Accessed December 7, 2016.

Biskupic, Joan. "Ginsburg: Court Needs Another Woman." *USA Today,* May 5, 2009. usatoday30.usatoday.com/news/washington/judicial/2009-05-05-ruthginsburg_N.htm. Accessed February 12, 2017.

Boorstein, Michelle. "Ruth Bader Ginsburg Calls for Equal Rights Amendment to the Constitution." *Washington Post,* February 2, 2018. www.washingtonpost.com/news/acts-of-faith/wp/2018/02/02/carrying-an-i-dissent-tote-bag-on-stage-ruth-bader-ginsburg-tells-d-c-crowd-shes-still-going-full-steam/?utm_term=.0c45b017fac4. Accessed February 10, 2018.

Bucklo, Elaine. "Rules to Live By: From Women's Rights Advocate to Supreme Court Justice: Ruth Bader Ginsburg Speaks." *Litigation* (American Bar Association) 37, no. 2 (Winter 2011).

Burritt, Kelsey. "Justice Ginsburg to Speak on Two Great Passions: Law, Opera." *Chautauquan Daily,* July 28, 2013. chqdaily.wordpress.com/2013/07/28/justice-ginsburg-to-speak-on-two-great-passions-law-opera. Accessed August 17, 2016.

Campbell, Linda P., and Linda M. Harrington. "Judge Ruth Bader Ginsburg: Portrait of a 'Steel Butterfly.'" *Chicago Tribune,* June 27, 1993. articles.chicagotribune.com/1993-06-27/news/9306270324_1_judge-ruth-bader-ginsburg-supreme-court-harvard-law-school. Accessed October 3, 2016.

Carlson, Margaret. "The Law According to Ruth." *Time,* June 28, 1993. content.time.com/time/magazine/article/0,9171,978785,00.html. Accessed June 23, 2016.

Carmon, Irin. "Exclusive Justice Ruth Bader Ginsburg Interview: Full Transcript." *The Rachel Maddow Show,* February 16, 2015. www.msnbc.com/msnbc/exclusive-justice-ruth-bader-ginsburg-interview-full-transcript. Accessed May 7, 2016.

———. "Justice Ginsburg's Cautious Radicalism." *New York Times,* October 24, 2015. www.nytimes.com/2015/10/25/opinion/sunday/justice-ginsburgs-cautious-radicalism.html?_r=0. Accessed August 7, 2016.

Cole, Sean. "The Man Who Builds the Bodies of the Law." *American Public Media,* June 26, 2013. www.thestory.org/stories/2013-06/man-who-builds-bodies-law. Accessed December 6, 2016.

Donadio, Rachel. "Justice Ruth Bader Ginsburg Presides Over Shylock's Appeal." *New York Times,* July 27, 2016. www.nytimes.com/2016/07/28/theater/ruth-bader-ginsburg-rbg-venice-merchant-of-venice.html. Accessed September 4, 2016.

Epstein, Nadine. "Ruth Bader Ginsburg: 'The Notorious RBG.'" *Moment Magazine,* May–June 2015. www.momentmag.com/ruth-bader-ginsburg-notorious-rbg-interview. Accessed July 12, 2016.

Frauenheim, Ed. "Lilly Ledbetter Interview: 'Miss Lilly' Speaks Her Mind." *Workforce,* August 21, 2012. www.workforce.com/2012/08/21/lilly-ledbetter-interview-miss-lilly-speaks-her-mind. Accessed December 12, 2016.

Frederick, Joe. "Joe's Story." *Strike the Root,* November 16, 2003. www.strike-the-root.com. Accessed May 1, 2016.

Galanes, Philip. "Ruth Bader Ginsburg and Gloria Steinem on the Unending Fight for Women's Rights." *New York Times,* November 14, 2015. www.nytimes.com/2015/11/15/fashion/ruth-bader-ginsburg-and-gloria-steinem-on-the-unending-fight-for-womens-rights.html. Accessed October 18, 2016.

Garner, Bryan A. "Ruth Bader Ginsburg." In *The Scribes Journal of Legal Writing.* Lansing, Michigan: Scribes—American Society of Legal Writers, 2010, 133.

Ginsburg, Martin D. "A Uniquely Distinguished Service." *Green Bag,* 10, no. 2 (Winter 2007): 173–76.

Ginsburg, Ruth Bader. "A Conversation with Ruth Bader Ginsburg, Associate Justice of the United States Supreme Court." The Tanner Lectures in Human Values. University of Michigan. February 6, 2015. tannerlectures.utah.edu/Ginsburg%20manuscript.pdf. Accessed August 14, 2016.

———. "Alumni Spotlight: Ruth Bader Ginsburg '59." *Columbia Law School Magazine* (Winter 2010): 80. www.law.columbia.edu/sites/default/files/microsites/magazine/files/c_winter_2010.pdf. Accessed September 12, 2016.

———. "Independence." In *What I Told My Daughter: Lessons from Leaders on Raising the Next Generation of Empowered Women,* edited by Nina Tassler. New York: Atria Books, 2016, 113–17.

———. "My First Opera." Opera America. July 13, 2015. medium.com/my-first-opera/justice-ruth-bader-ginsburg-and-justice-antonin-scalia-as-superumeraries-in-washington-national-2d802e1d6f95#.dkxr1azff. Accessed May 23, 2016.

. *My Own Words.* New York: Simon and Schuster, 2016.

———. "Prefaces to *Scalia/Ginsburg:* A (Gentle) Parody of Operatic Proportions." *Columbia Journal of Law and Arts* 38, no. 2 (2015): 237.

———. "Remarks for the American Law Institute Annual Dinner." C-SPAN. May 19, 1994. www.c-span.org/video/?56906-1/supreme-court-perspective. Accessed June 12, 2016.

Gluck, Abbe R. "A Conversation with Justice Ruth Bader Ginsburg." *Faculty Scholarship Series.* Paper 4905. Yale Law School Legal Scholarship Repository, 2013, 7.

Goldberg, Stephanie B. "The Second Woman Justice: Ruth Bader Ginsburg Talks Candidly About a Changing Society." *ABA Journal* 79, no. 19 (October 1993): 40–43.

Halper, Daniel. "Justice Ginsburg on Working Out." *Weekly Standard,* March 20, 2013. www.weeklystandard.com/justice-ginsburg-on-working-out-when-i-started-i-looked-like-a-survivor-of-auschwitz/article/708719. Accessed July 6, 2017.

Harrington, Mona. *Women Lawyers: Rewriting the Rules.* New York: Plume, 1995.

Hewitt, Bill. "Feeling Supreme." *People,* June 28, 1993. people.com/archive/feeling-supreme-vol-39-no-25. Accessed January 19, 2017.

Hirshman, Linda. *Sisters in Law.* New York: HarperCollins, 2015.

Kay, Herma Hill. "Claiming a Space in the Law School Curriculum: A Casebook on Sex-Based Discrimination." *Columbia Journal of Gender and Law* 25, no. 1 (2013): 54–62.

Labaton, Stephen. "The Man Behind the High Court Nominee." *New York Times,* June 17, 1993. www.nytimes.com/1993/06/17/us/the-man-behind-the-high-court-nominee.html. Accessed July 26, 2016.

Lamb, Brian, Susan Swain, and Mark Farkas, eds. "Justice Ruth Bader Ginsburg." In *The Supreme Court: A C-SPAN Book Featuring the Justices in Their Own Words.* New York: PublicAffairs, 2010, 106–21.

Lewis, John. "Note to Self." *CBS This Morning.* CBS News. June 29, 2017. www.cbsnews.com/news/note-to-self-congressman-john-lewis-civil-rights-leader. Accessed June 30, 2017.

Lewis, John, and Michael D'Orso. *Walking with the Wind: A Memoir of the Movement.* New York: Harcourt Brace & Co., 1999.

Margolick, David. "Trial by Adversity Shapes Jurist's Outlook." *New York Times,* June 25, 1993. www.nytimes.com/1993/06/25/us/trial-by-adversity-shapes-jurist-s-outlook. html?pagewanted=all. Accessed May 17, 2016.

Mathews, Jay. "The Spouse of Ruth." *Washington Post,* June 19, 1993. www.washingtonpost. com/archive/lifestyle/1993/06/19/the-spouse-of-ruth/a57e6536-3e1b-4c30-8bab-1f2c629cf172/?utm_term=.f1931486fe1b. Accessed July 2, 2016.

Mayeri, Serena. "'When the Trouble Started': The Story of *Frontiero v. Richardson.*" U of Penn Law School, Public Law Research Paper no. 10–13. February 4, 2011. In *Women and the Law Stories,* edited by Elizabeth Schneider and Stephanie M. Wildman. Foundation Press, 2011. papers.ssrn.com/sol3/papers.cfm?abstract_id=1583064. Accessed April 22, 2016.

Merritt, Deborah Jones, and Wendy Webster Williams. "Transcript of Interview of U.S. Supreme Court Associate Justice Ruth Bader Ginsburg, April 10, 2009." *Ohio State Law Journal* 70, no. 4 (2009): 805–25.

NPR Staff. "Ginsburg and Scalia: 'Best Buddies.'" *All Things Considered.* NPR. February 15, 2016. www.npr.org/2016/02/15/466848775/scalia-ginsburg-opera-commemorates-sparring-supreme-court-friendship. Accessed June 3, 2016.

O'Neill, Anne-Marie. "Not Going Quietly." *People,* March 10, 1997. people.com/archive/not-going-quietly-vol-47-no-9/feed. Accessed December 18, 2016.

Pogrebin, Abigail. "In Chambers with Ruth Bader Ginsburg." *Moment Magazine,* February 2006. www.momentmag.com/wp-content/uploads/2013/03/In-Chambers-with-Ruth-Bader-Ginsburg.pdf. Accessed August 23, 2016.

———. *Stars of David: Prominent Jews Talk About Being Jewish.* New York: Broadway Books, 2005, 18–24.

Pogrebin, Letty Cottin. "The Working Woman: Mothers Who Raise Successful Daughters." *Ladies' Home Journal,* May 1979. Ruth Bader Ginsburg Papers, Library of Congress, Box 19, Miscellany, Biographical File, 1979–1980. Accessed March 24, 2017.

Rosen, Jeffrey. "Ruth Bader Ginsburg Is an American Hero." *New Republic,* September 28, 2014.

Saline, Carol, and Sharon J. Wohlmuth. *Mothers and Daughters.* New York: Doubleday, 1997, 48–51.

Sandalow, Marc. "Ruth Bader Ginsburg at UCDC." University of California: Washington Center. October 27, 2014. www.ucdc.edu/ruth-bader-ginsburg-ucdc. Accessed June 23, 2017.

Sarfati, Susan. "Lilly Ledbetter, the Woman Behind the Fair Pay Act." *PCMA Convene,* June 1, 2014. www.pcmaconvene.org/features/lilly-ledbetter-the-woman-behind-the-fair-pay-act. Accessed December 13, 2016.

Saulnier, Beth. "Justice Prevails: A Conversation with Ruth Bader Ginsburg '54." *Cornell Alumni Magazine,* November–December 2013: 40–45. cornellalumnimagazine.com/justice-prevails. Accessed December 17, 2016.

Schatz, Phil. "Judicial Profile: Hon. Ruth Bader Ginsburg." *Federal Lawyer,* May 2010. www.wsfny.com/phils-book-reviews/90-judicial-profile-hon-ruth-bader-ginsberg.html. Accessed May 13, 2016.

Schlanger, Margo. "Five Former Clerks Share Thoughts About Justice Ginsburg." *Law Quadrangle: Notes from Michigan Law,* Spring 2015. quadrangle.law.umich.edu/spring2015/umichlaw/5-former-clerks-share-thoughts-about-justice-ginsburg. Accessed July 1, 2017.

Swiger, Elinor Porter. "Ruth Bader Ginsburg." *Women Lawyers at Work.* New York: Julian Messner, 1978, 50–66.

Tassler, Nina. *What I Told My Daughter: Lessons from Leaders in Raising the Next Generation of Empowered Women.* New York: Atria Books, 2016.

Thomas, Marlo, and Friends. "The Honorable Ruth Bader Ginsburg." *The Right Words at the Right Time.* New York: Atria Books, 2002, 115–17.

Toohey, Joe. "Brooklyn School's Many Famous Alumni." *Fox 5 News,* May 12, 2016. www.fox5ny.com/news/140429442-story. Accessed July 12, 2016.

Von Drehle, David. "Conventional Roles Hid a Revolutionary Intellect." *Washington Post,* July 18, 1993. www.washingtonpost.com/archive/politics/1993/07/18/conventional-roles-hid-a-revolutionary-intellect/38a8055a-d575-4eee-b59a-44c2d58771f5/?utm_term=.8d42ef5b53c9. Accessed May 14, 2016.

———. "Redefining Fair with a Simple Careful Assault." *Washington Post,* July 19, 1993. www.washingtonpost.com/archive/politics/1993/07/19/redefining-fair-with-a-simple-careful-assault/3a57e57b-ed36-46e9-a2e1-f10fc8b004be/?utm_term=.ef6e7b317c14. Accessed May 27, 2016.

Vrato, Elizabeth. *The Counselors: Conversations with 18 Courageous Women Who Have Changed the World.* Philadelphia: Running Press, 2002, 173–85.

Ward, Stephanie Francis. "Family Ties." *ABA Journal,* October 2010. www.abajournal.com/magazine/article/family_ties1. Accessed April 24, 2016.

"What Lilly Ledbetter Wants Women to Know About Equal Pay." *Self,* January 29, 2016. www.self.com/story/lilly-ledbetter-equal-pay-interview. Accessed December 12, 2016.

PHOTO CREDITS

Reuters, Stephen Crowley/*The New York Times:* 87

The Richard Avedon Foundation. Photograph by Richard Avedon © 2007. Courtesy of the Collection of the Supreme Court of the United States: 104

Ruth Bader Ginsburg Papers, Part I: Box 21, Manuscript Division, Library of Congress, Washington, D.C.: 80

Scott Suchman: 157

U.S. Air Force: 132

INDEX

Note: Page references in **bold** indicate photos and their captions.